SCALING YOUR BUSINESS

with

MOD

VIRTUAL
PROFESSIONALS

SCALING YOUR BUSINESS

with

MOD

VIRTUAL PROFESSIONALS

HOW TO DRIVE **REVENUE**, SAVE **TIME**, AND CREATE YOUR **DREAM COMPANY**

DANIEL **RAMSEY**

Acknowledgments

To my loving wife. Every day I get to walk into my office at 8:00 a.m. and kick ass in business and know, without a doubt, that everything in my personal world is handled because of Whitney Ramsey. Whitney, you are, 100 percent, the rock on which our family's happiness and love stand. Thank you for all that you do for us. You've tolerated my unrelenting drive to improve and level up every aspect of our lives.

To my lovely, young daughters, Georgia and June, I'll always be your biggest fan and most ardent supporter of your dreams!

To the MyOutDesk virtual professionals: I love you all, truly. I admire your daily dedication to our mission of being indispensable to our clients. Every day, I'm reminded of the amazing business you have built and all the positive impact you've made in the world.

To our five thousand clients and the MOD Movement founding members: Wow, what a ride it has been! We have had ten years worth of positivity and love. Thank you for your support and for trusting us to help scale your business. Your monthly subscriptions and charitable contributions have created true impact in a world! Your contributions will provide opportunity and hope that will change the course of thousands of lives.

The MyOutDesk team celebrates at MODCon.

To the readers of this book: I've spent the last twelve years pouring my heart and soul into the business and clients that we serve. That blood, that sweat, those tears are represented here in a book of best practices for your journey to grow and scale your business. I trust you will find value here!

Daniel

CONTENTS

Prologue

"If I could build a business, what kind would I build?" As a child, I spent an inordinate amount of time pondering that question. I didn't like growing up poor, so my fantasy was to travel the world as a businessman.

I had a good work ethic as a kid and even gained some practical business experience early on. When I was in high school, my economics teacher told me that if you are born poor, you'll almost certainly be poor as an adult. I was 100 percent confident that I would prove him wrong. After all, I'd already started earning money.

Back in 1990, I had a monopoly selling candy on the Sequoia Middle School bus. (See figure 1.) I was enjoying an unusual stroke of luck: the Shasta County School Board had banned the sale of soda and candy at all area schools the previous summer. Sugar, they say, is a powerful drug, and I quickly earned a steady supply of customers. (Being the father of a three-year-old and five-year-old today, I have renewed understanding of the power of a good bar of chocolate.)

My motivation was not bucking the system or making new friends. It was money, plain and simple. I grew up in a trailer park without disposable income. I had to find, or make my own, side hustles because my friends had money to go to the movies or out to lunch, and I didn't want to miss out. I can extrapolate this motivation out to my life even today. All the financial and global impact I've had can be traced to an inner hunger to be more financially successful than my parents, and to make a difference in the world. To simply matter.

But I bring up my candy business on that bus not just because it's an example of one of my earliest understandings of meeting demand but because it was my earliest understanding of *supply* and demand. On that bouncing bus, something happened that forever changed my life.

Summers in Redding, California, are notoriously hot, and the school year was almost over. On that Friday home from school, I had one Snickers left in my backpack. While I generally followed the rule all successful drug dealers abide by—"never sample the goods"—today was different. It was the last day of the week, and I had sold more than $100 worth of candy. I was rich! Plus, I hadn't had any expenses. I'd bought shoes the month before, and the Snickers bar was being perfectly warmed by that sun. So, I was going to eat that chocolate without one bit, or bite, of guilt.

Daniel's Childhood Hustle

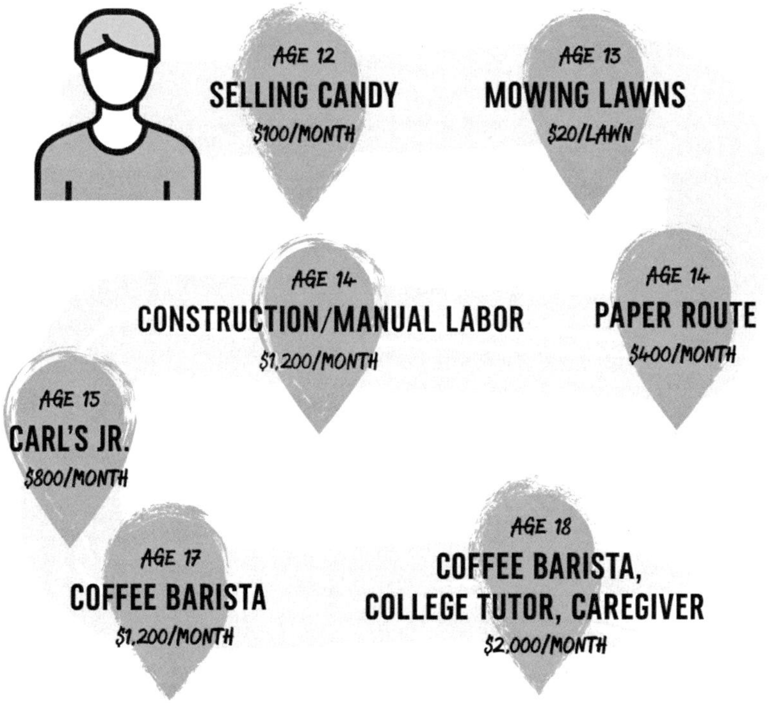

Figure 1. Before I started college, I'd had several jobs, all found or developed by me, and each building on a growing skill set.

I sat sideways with my back to the cool breeze from a window at the back of the bus and was just about to pull the candy from my bag. A kid named John scooted next to me.

"Daniel, do you have any more Snickers?" he asked.

Now, my parents raised me to be honest, and at that age, I didn't have a poker face. So, I responded the only way I knew how.

"Come on, John," I sighed. "I haven't had any candy all week, and I was saving this last one for myself. It's warm, so the chocolate will melt perfectly in my mouth. Sorry, I can't sell it to you."

John bargained with me, first offering me two dollars, which was twice the usual rate for one candy bar, then five dollars. When I stuck to my guns, he said something that blew my mind.

"I'll give you twenty dollars for it! Give it to me right now!"

That moment sealed my fate. I knew I was going to sell things for a living. Moreover, I had witnessed in action the primary law of business: supply and demand. In seventh grade, I got a small glimpse into the driver for all levels of business. (And by the way, as soon as I got off the bus, I went to the store and bought another Snickers bar for twenty-five cents!) That day, I became a serial entrepreneur; I was drawn to and had a natural love for business.

I continued learning the principles of business with a lawn care business and a paper route. Shortly after I graduated from college, I launched a real estate company. It was my first experience of a multimillion-dollar business, but more importantly, it was my introduction into how to start and build a truly successful business: not by just using the power of supply and demand but by scaling and selling. This led me to innovate the 7-Figure Business Roadmap, my unique, step-by-step process to building a seven-figure business.

In the real estate game, it's almost impossible to build a business that is saleable. Only 11 percent of people who obtain a real estate license earn a living selling real estate, and only a very small percentage of those ever sell their businesses. As I learned about the industry, I quickly realized I had to be a buyer of the product I was selling, or I'd have no way of building assets. I'm happy to report that after fourteen years of being in the real estate game, I was able to sell my real-estate investment business for millions of dollars.

As I built my real estate company, I also started another venture, a company called MyOutDesk. Our goal as a company is to provide indispensable virtual professionals to businesses that want to scale. We are now in our twelfth year of operation, and I'm so proud of the work we've accomplished as a company. Our work at MyOutDesk has truly changed the world; we've been honored to serve more than four thousand companies in North America. Having those businesses as clients has been a massive source of pride for the MyOutDesk team, and you can imagine what it's like to have thousands of people's lives impacted with high-paying jobs and hope for their families' futures.

This book is going to demystify the process of growing a company from zero to netting a $1 million a year with what we call the 7-Figure Business Roadmap. A simple fact about business models is that there is typically a step-by-step process of growth. Each stage of that growth represents a new challenge and a shift in mindset. I've identified those stages, and this book will articulate the climb as if I am your guide as you are climbing Mount Everest.

As the cofounder and CEO of MyOutDesk, I have been able to witness so many different growth paths in a variety of industries with different business models. It has been an amazing experience to watch patterns emerge as my team and I helped more than four thousand businesses scale with virtual professionals. Times are indeed changing, and the model we employ at MyOutDesk is far too impactful not to share. If you are interested in making an impact in the world and creating a seven-figure business along the way, this book is for you.

I'm excited about the Scale Your Business with Virtual Professionals journey we're about to embark on together!

David

The Story of How I Scaled My Business

Of all the places I could have had an epiphany about my business, mine hit me on my honeymoon.

In 2009, my new bride and I were honeymooning in Guatemala. We were staying at La Lancha, Francis Ford Coppola's magically romantic lakeside resort nestled in the rainforest. We had spent an idyllic day hiking through the jungle and scrambling through the ruins of the ancient city of Tikal. It was breathtaking.

Inspired but exhausted, we went back to our hotel, had dinner, and did what newlyweds do. But once my wife was asleep, I crept down to the bar to work.

Yes, to work.

At the time, I had been using virtual professionals (VPs)[1] in my real estate business for about two years. These are full-time, part-time, contract, and freelance workers who work from their home offices around the world. Yet there I was acting like my own VP, at two o'clock in the morning, in the bar closing deals, on my honeymoon. Why? Because at that time, I was the only person in the office who could generate revenue. I had VPs handling administrative, marketing, and sales support for my real estate company. What I didn't have was someone with a real estate license who knew how to generate business, to take a deal from start to finish, and to collect revenue for the company.

I did this for a few nights, and the bartender noticed. My Spanish wasn't great at the time, but I knew he was making fun of me. My beautiful bride was abandoned in our room, already a laptop widow. Suddenly, the sheer ridiculousness of my situation hit me like a ton of bricks.

The Chinese have a kanji character for the word "busy" that is a combination of the characters for "heart" plus "killing." Perhaps this is a subtle bit of wisdom hidden in the language, but for me *busy* really was starting to equal death. I was thirty pounds heavier than I am today and had heart-attack-level blood pressure. I was working all the time because I thought I had to have a hand in everything in my business. In my head, I couldn't shut business off to fully enjoy anything, not even my honeymoon. But in that moment in the hotel bar, I realized it was harming my health, mind, and body. I knew that if I wanted to be present for my wife and one day have a family, I needed to make a new roadmap for my business, and I needed it quick. I flew home from Guatemala with a new resolve to build a business that could scale, work without me when I needed it to, and one day, be saleable.

Busy = Heart + Killing

Over the last ten years, my company has revamped everything in our business model. It was as if we got rid of an old computer and got a new one with a new operating system. It was a clean slate and a completely new way of thinking—one that included us hiring five thousand VPs.

---

1. In this book, I use "virtual professional" (VP) and "virtual assistant" (VA) interchangeably. I also refer to these employees as "freelancers." But I far and above prefer VP, and I explain why in chapter 7.

It took two years to build my three companies up to a point where I felt comfortable leaving them for a time and having them run without me. In 2011, I did just that. My wife and I moved to Peru for six months, and while we were there, the businesses continued to grow and make money for us from a distance. We rented an apartment there, got involved in our community, joined a gym, and learned Spanish for four hours a day. Have you ever wanted to immerse yourself in another culture, to live like the locals? We were able to travel to five different countries while experiencing everything South America has to offer, from the Inca Trail, to the vineyards of Mendoza in Argentina, to surfing in North Chile, while generating lots of cash. For the first time in my career, I had leapfrogged my peers, who were back home stuck in the daily grind.

> The 7-Figure Business Roadmap gives you a scalable business that doesn't require the owner to be in the day-to-day operations and that is saleable!

We lived, earned money, and grew our net worth, all while using the MyOutDesk system I will share with you in this book. Using The 7-Figure Business Roadmap, the Scale Community, and our various frameworks and scale accelerators, you will learn how to hire VPs and then empower them to grow, so your business can scale. Having developed this system through sheer necessity and a lot of trial and error, I am sharing it with you the easy way so that you can simply "download" it. I also provide links to our website and resources throughout the book.

Leveraging Global Talent

A note about staying true to fair business practices: As you will read in this book, it is important for you to know that VPs are not just people, often from abroad, who can work for a more price-competitive salary than the alternative. While it is true that it is possible to pay them less than we do for a similar job here in this country, these are talented, intelligent people with great English and a fantastic work ethic who we can leverage through the principle of currency arbitrage. To give an example of what currency arbitrage is, when I was living in Peru, a taxi ride cost one dollar, whereas that same ride would cost ten dollars in America. Similarly, in the USA, a bottle of water costs two dollars, but it would cost only twenty cents in Peru. By hiring VPs from abroad, you are saving money while also providing someone with a highly competitive wage that reflects his or her talents and work ethic at a price your business can afford. As a businessperson, you can hire a full-time sales professional, marketing professional, or administrative professional very reasonably this way.

Our Journey Begins

Now it is time to embark on the Scale with Virtual Professionals journey. After you read this book, you will be able to do the following:

1. Scale your business using virtual professionals.
2. Use MyOutDesk's scale accelerators to achieve high growth.
3. Implement scale frameworks right now to win you more time-freedom in your life, more sales for your business, and more passion for your business.
4. Discover the Scale Community for support on your Scale Your Business with Virtual Professionals journey.

To help you along the way, visit our website, https://www.MyOutDesk.com.

Specifically, see:
https://www.MyOutDesk.com/Framework
https://www.MyOutDesk.com/Accelerator
https://www.MyOutDesk.com/Community

The MyOutDesk brand promise:

We instantly scale growing companies with virtual professionals.

Chapter 1

The Future Is Blended: The Argument for Virtual Professionals

Engine revved? Hand on the gearshift? Seat belt on? (What? Don't all Steve McQueens take time to strap in?) OK, download your 7-Figure Business Roadmap (https://www.MyOutDesk.com/7FigureBusinessRoadmap; also in chapter 5, starting on page 26), and let's begin yourscaling journey. Whether your current business is large or small, it's important that you understand two things before you begin to scale: where you are and where you are going.

Pros Only and the 7-Figure Business Roadmap

Business and sports provide very similar experiences for people who want to be champions and win. In any high school sport, there's a coach and perhaps a couple of assistant coaches, a workout discipline, a required practice schedule, and matches to test your team's ability against the competition's. In business, the exact same systems exist. You can have a coach, a workout discipline, and daily practice routines, and then you get to be in front of clients fighting for the business.

The 7-Figure Business Roadmap simply describes, for business owners, what is equivalent to the differences among competing in high school, college, and the pros. It's a clear articulation of the player's landscape: the challenges, key drivers, and team member rosters. The Business Roadmap will help you focus on the things that matter at different levels of *revenue* and *team size*. If you dream about playing in your industry's version of the NFL, come get the 7-Figure Business Roadmap, so while you're in college or even high school, you can practice like you're going pro.

Scale Accelerator: Model what the pros do daily! Replicate the workout and practice discipline and the client-acquisition model of the giant in your industry. Visit https://www.MyOutDesk.com /Accelerator.

Leverage = Profit

There are about 28 million businesses in the United States. According to the US Small Business Administration, all but about 20,000 of those are small businesses—that is, they have fewer than 500 employees.[1] That means that 99 percent of businesses nationwide are considered "small." Eighty percent, more than 22 million, of those small businesses are non-employers, meaning they have zero employees. The other 6 million or so do have employees. According to the US Census Bureau, of all small businesses with employees, only 4 percent have managed to scale to the extent that they net $1 million per year.[2] (See figure 2.)

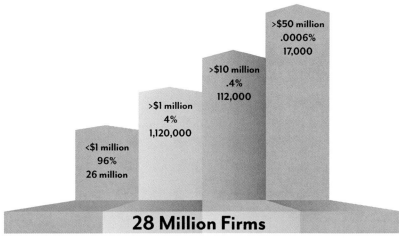

Figure 2. According to IRS, there are a total of 28 million firms in the US, and of those firms, only 4 percent earn over a million dollars.

---

1. Schwinn, Richard. "2016 State Small Business Profiles Released with Fresh Design." *The Small Business Advocate*, March–April 2016, www.sba.gov/sites/default/files/March_April_2016 _FINAL_508_compliant.pdf.

2. "Small Business." https://www.census.gov/smallbusiness.

This seeming reluctance to use employees to grow businesses represents lost opportunity of epic proportions for US business owners. Perhaps this trend is perpetuated because it is so tempting to slip into the mindset that taking on employees is too expensive and training them (and managing them on a daily basis) is too time-consuming. Business owners often think that things would just be easier if they did it all themselves and that taking on the responsibility of employees is too much of a gamble. Yet the truth is quite the opposite. Statistically speaking, when an entrepreneur takes on even a handful of employees, profits soar. The annual average sales of a company with one employee (sole proprietorships) total $47,000; with four employees, that number becomes $387,000. That is, when the number of employees increases by a factor of four, profits increase by a factor of eight. The numbers don't lie. Bottom line, hiring employees can dramatically increase your profits.

You Were Born at a Time of Historic Opportunity

If you are alive today (having caught you in the act of reading, I suspect you are), you have enormous good fortune. The fact that the internet and other modernizations have globalized our economy gives you a chance to scale your business faster and further than ever before, using VPs who may work around the world from you. This is the blended employment model that is harnessing the power of this digital era and using it for good—your business's good.

It is my mission to ensure that you don't miss that opportunity. If you choose to take your business up the value chain toward netting $1 million a year, know that it really isn't rocket science. The tools, tactics, and frameworks I am going to introduce you to are not some new craze or a passing fad; they are tried-and-true, statistically proven frameworks that have worked for many in the past. The path from being a solo business owner to being an owner of a small- or even medium-sized business does not have to be mysterious or convoluted. It is a path many have taken before, and this book can be your guidepost as you go.

The heart of the journey is getting the right people working for you. The ability to leverage global talent makes it financially attainable, even for smaller companies, to do so. America's biggest companies already know this, as we are beginning to discover.

Economic Titans Leverage Talent Globally

Large companies are benefiting from using a blended employment model. In fact, a new regulation stemming from the Dodd-Frank Wall Street

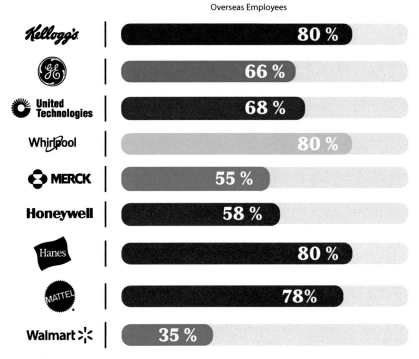

Figure 3.

Reform and Consumer Protection Act has given us a clearer picture of the extent to which some of the largest US companies employ global talent. As part of this act, publicly traded companies are now required to disclose how many foreign employees they have. While this act was passed back in 2010 in response to the 2008 global financial crisis, the SEC (Securities and Exchange Commission) approved implementation and compliance guidance for companies only in September 2017.

Therefore, data regarding the degree to which these major corporations use global talent is only beginning to emerge, but the numbers are sizeable. Even after just one quarter of such reporting, it is clear that many of the most recognizable US brands hire workers in lower-cost countries as a means of leveraging their businesses. One of the reasons this has been hitting the news of late is that publicly traded companies are also required to disclose CEO pay ratios, the difference between what the CEO of a company is paid and what that company's median worker earns. Since an increasing number of companies are hiring in lower-cost countries, some of those figures astound the average reader.

You might be surprised at the high percentages of global talent that successful companies have reported so far. (See figure 3.)

These are 2018 figures, which represent a handful of first-quarter-reporting companies' percentages. As time goes on, we will see more and more companies reporting on the success of their blended organizational models, in which employees in the United States have their roles within their areas of strength, and employees abroad have others. What these major corporations are finding is that there is a lot of revenue to be saved by offering job opportunities in lower-cost nations. You should too, because if you don't, you are missing a large opportunity. (See figure 2.)

Harness the Power of the Virtual Workforce

As a Deloitte study found in 2017, only 13 percent of US employees are passionate about their jobs.[3] The nation's workforce is ready for what Steve Jones, author of *Virtual Culture*, called a "corporate detox." As millennial and technological changes continue to influence the way companies work—and what employees want and expect to counter that dissatisfaction—we can see a shift toward what Accenture has dubbed a "liquid" workforce composed of VPs who work mostly from home. Accenture predicts that by 2020, 43 percent of Americans will be VPs.[4]

Demand for virtual talent is increasing because it works for most business owners and many employees, and it is simply a profitable practice. Let this book be a guide for how to do it the right way. Meanwhile, the global, virtual-talent market is rapidly expanding; in some estimates, this market will be worth over 6 billion US dollars by 2021. These, in addition to our desire to impact the world, are the changing forces that have influenced the way we work at MyOutDesk. With these factors in mind, I have crafted this path for you with a bird's-eye view from the top of the metaphorical mountain I have scaled with my own businesses. From this perspective, I can see the clearest, simplest, and fastest path for you toward a million-dollar business in the current economic climate, so there is no

---

3. Hagel, John, John Seely Brown, Maggie Wooll, and Alok Ranjan. "If You Love Them Set Them Free." *Deloitte Insights*, June 6, 2017, https://www2.deloitte.com/us/en/insights/topics/talent/future-workforce-engagement-in-the-workplace.html.

4. "Trend 2: Liquid Workforce: Building the Workforce for Today's Digital Demands." *Accenture*, 2016, https://www.accenture.com/fr-fr/_acnmedia/pdf-2/accenture-liquid-workforce-technology-vision-2016-france.pdf

need to navigate the crevices and rockslides. This book will be your guide and your source of clarity in this brave new business world.

You've waited long enough. Now that we have assessed the scene, let's open the map and find out where you are on it.

Chapter 2
The "I Do It" Stage

Borrowing terminology from video gaming, figuring out how to "level up" your business may seem daunting while you are in the midst of your day-to-day grind. But the truth is, the steps involved are standard steps; each business goes through them. The difficult part for business owners is gaining perspective, being able to zoom out far enough to see these steps in the context of the whole 7-Figure Business Roadmap. That is precisely what we will do in the next three chapters. We will begin by taking in an aerial view, so you can see where you are on the map, from a newbie making no money to the seasoned pro netting a million dollars a year. That will give you the ability to determine what stage your business is in and what you need to do next for it to grow.

The destination, as I've mentioned before, is to put yourself in a position to make a bigger impact in the world; have "time-freedom," or ownership of your minutes, hours, and days, to live a life worth living; and build value in your business, so you can have an asset to sell if you get hurt or sick, grow tired of the industry you are in, or simply wish to retire.

If you are an entrepreneur creating value in the world, there should be a payoff at the end. The problem is that many business owners don't realize they may be sabotaging their endgame because they are stuck in an ownership mentality; their business is their baby. That mindset will keep your business stuck, and as I describe the three stages of business—each with two substages, which we'll get into in chapter 5—you will see how letting go of the ownership mentality is your first step toward success. For the next three chapters, let's stick to the main three stages, as summarized in figure 4:

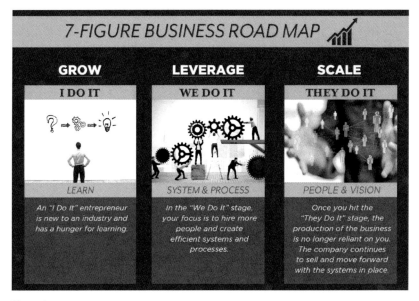

Figure 4.

All entrepreneurial ventures start from the beginning, and this chapter focuses on the first stage: the "I Do It" solopreneur.

The I Do It Stage

There is a lot of excitement in the I Do It stage. I Do It entrepreneurs are new to an industry and have a hunger for learning. Their business is indeed their baby, and they think, "I built it, and it works for me." Which is fine in the beginning. Most of the time, they are solopreneurs, meaning they do the work themselves. They are also often in the process of learning how to solve a problem and to be compensated based on how big that problem is (the market) and how well they solve it (the value proposition). They are really in the process of "becoming."

The upside for I Do Its is their overhead is low, and most of the revenue the business makes goes right to them. At this stage, there are no or few employees to provide for. What the I Do Its need to learn is how to get a deeper understanding of their industry, how to generate revenue, who their clients are, and what their value proposition is out on the market.

Even though I am no longer at the I Do It stage, I can fully appreciate the feeling of having a business baby. As I have already shared, my early employment experiences turned me off working for other people completely. I was a born entrepreneur; if I was going to make money for someone, that someone was going to be me. I wanted to control my own destiny. If you have a business yourself, you probably feel the same. Most entrepreneurs will do anything it takes to stay in the driver's seat when it comes to their prosperity.

Real estate was the ideal place for me to embark from as a solo entrepreneur because the barriers to entry were not high. You simply got a license and started doing it. There were no capital expenditures, and it was a business that was very easy to understand. I had a good network and was not too worried about starting up, but for me, the biggest cost was going to be getting an office. I feel like I have a unique perspective to offer to solopreneurs because not only did I start off solo in 2004 but I had to start over again just four years later. This wasn't because my business had failed; in fact, even though I was in my early twenties and largely engaged in self-educating in business at the time, I had quickly built a company with several employees. But I had been lucky. I had entered the real estate market when it was hot.

That wasn't the case in 2007, when the financial crisis hit. Then, real estate was a catastrophic place to be. The market had full-on crashed. Residential real estate and commercial real estate had been humming along like a car driving down the freeway, and then it seemed like, in an instant, somebody put up a wall that was ten feet thick and twenty yards wide. Ninety percent of my business revenue stopped, all in a ninety-day period.

In December 2006, my business had a month's net profit of $80,000, which was great. That's a snapshot of where I was at that point: I was on top of the world.

Conversely, for the whole first quarter of 2007, we made a profit of $7,000 (more than a 90 percent drop in revenue).

There was no question about what had to happen next: I had to let go of every employee who was not bringing in revenue, those who were non-dollar-productive. There was just no other answer. First, all the front office staff went, and then, as a month or two passed, all the agents had to go because no one was selling anything. It was hard to do. I had it better than some, however. I didn't go bankrupt. From that moment, I was a solopreneur again. I was back doing everything on my own, from paperwork to prospecting to closing, and I worked my butt off. I was forced to move my office into my home. I had fourteen-hour days and worked weekends. If someone wanted to sell or buy real estate, I was talking to him or her personally.

I had a tempting job offer from an agency at that time, so I could have thrown in the towel if I wanted to become an employee again. But again I was lucky. I was twenty-eight, did not yet have a wife or kids, and was determined to maintain my independence in business. I was humbled but still hungry. I remember being at my new girlfriend's house for dinner that Easter. We were all dressed in our Sunday best, and I had just met her parents for the first time. We were outside talking and having fun when I got a call on my cell phone. It was a client with whom I was in the middle of negotiating a multimillion-dollar deal. I said, "Excuse me, I'll be right back," and walked away to take the call. Even though it was Easter Sunday, we had to have a conversation because the next day was the deadline for our deal.

My girlfriend's father (who is now my father-in-law) said after I returned to the party, "Jeez! Do you really have to work on Easter Sunday?"

"Pat," I said, "if I don't answer the phone, somebody else will."

That, in a nutshell, is the plight of the solopreneur. You're always on duty, alone.

Despite the entire struggle I went through, I don't regret having had to revisit the I Do It stage one bit. I'm grateful for that opportunity because when the time was right for me to take on employees again, I was able to hire in a better way, which led to the 7-Figure Business Roadmap and the founding of MyOutDesk.

Chapter 3

The "We Do It" Stage

At MyOutDesk, we help a lot of businesses scale through the "We Do It" stage because the We Do Its have begun to focus on hiring people and creating efficient systems and processes, which is our forte. If your business is at this stage, you have already hired an assistant and perhaps another salesperson or whoever is a producer in your world. You are also trying to pinpoint how you've become successful, extract that from your mind, and put a system or process around it so that others can duplicate that success.

At the We Do It stage, there are a lot of small and tight-knit teams. You might rent an office at this stage and start building a name for yourself. You might become a little bit of a local celebrity along the way. You are networking a lot and have begun to impact your local community at a higher stage.

I tell people that in terms of difficulty, becoming an I Do It entrepreneur is like getting a four-year degree. Moving to the We Do It stage is more like getting a master's degree and a PhD all at the same time. It's not easy, but once you do it, you are truly building business value and a future asset worth selling on the open market.

Real-Life Success Story:
Moving Out of the I Do It Stage with Knolly Williams

Knolly Williams is a rare breed of entrepreneur who owns several different companies, all of them in different stages of development, and is a bestselling author, speaker, and trainer. In this example, I'm focusing on his tech business. When his sales had been flat for two years because his technology was five years old, he had to make some tough decisions. He would either have to invest more time in his technology business and put in personal cash to grow the company or let it dissipate out of relevance.

When we first started to talk, I discovered Knolly's major challenge in growing this technology company was his inability to find great talent to run the business who wanted neither part ownership nor a huge salary. He had several employees come and go over the years, and none of them had helped the company grow.

> **Knolly said:** "Most people believe money is the thing, but not me; I believe time is so much more valuable. That's why I love MyOutDesk; it has given me back my *time*!"

That inability to find a talented person to whom he could truly delegate kept Knolly stuck in the I Do It stage, which meant his business wasn't growing and he felt like he had to do everything himself. This kept him from focusing on his passion, which is speaking professionally and training business owners around the country.

Addressing Knolly's challenge was quite simple for MyOutDesk, even though it had felt insurmountable to him. We helped him hire people and taught him everything we know about hiring virtual professionals to scale his business. Since Knolly's product was a CRM (customer relationship management) application, what he needed, first and foremost, was someone with an IT (information technology) background who could be a true partner for him and who could run the business.

We introduced him to Chris, who is based in the Philippines. Chris has an IT degree and was looking to work for a business in which he could be deeply involved. Since he joined forces with Knolly, revenue has increased 20 percent year over year. The technology that Knolly thought had gone dormant has undergone development and will soon be available as an iOS app. Knolly and Chris now have been working together for four years, and we recently honored Chris as our top employee at MODCon, MyOutDesk's biannual conference. Chris says he enjoys his work so much he almost considers it a hobby. He is quick to point out: "You are lucky if you love what you do here in the Philippines. And I love what I do.

When I work, I consider the business to be my own. I feel like a partner to Knolly. My decisions are based on how best to grow the company, and that makes it simple."

Finding someone he can trust to delegate to has set Knolly free. Because of virtual professionals, Knolly is a CEO who has moved on to the next stage and now is enjoying both a record year in sales and time-freedom to live a beautiful life.

Chapter 4

The "They Do It" Stage

As you scale, your business will shift to the "They Do It" stage. It is an exciting place to be. The big difference between the We Do It stage and the They Do It stage is that at the They Do It stage, the production of the company is no longer reliant on only you, the owner. Freedom is born here. A They Do It entrepreneur can take a day or two off (or a whole month), and the business continues to sell and move forward with the systems in place.

This is not to say that you are no longer selling at this stage. You are still selling, but at this point, you are focusing on only the most major, game-changing deals. You're creating a channel of sales opportunities and strategic partnerships, and your employees are handling the day-to-day, transactional business.

Another big difference at this stage is that you are no longer chasing business. You have created a name for yourself and may even be well-known in your community, and that recognition for your name and company draws business in to you.

What sets the We Do Its and the They Do Its apart is not just the size of the company or the number of employees but rather the creation of an independent company culture. You will have given your employees a feeling that by working for you, they are doing more than simply putting money in your bank account. Your employees will believe in your mission and vision, which includes giving back to your community and the world.

My "They Do It" Baptism by Fire

My own move from the We Do It to the They Do It stage with my real estate company was a bit radical. We will talk about the 7-Figure Business Roadmap's substages in the next chapter, but spoiler alert: I skipped one of them.

My impetus for making such a dramatic change in my business was my move to Peru for six months. In order to prepare for that, I had to fully document our sales, delivery, and financial-management processes. Although I was going to have access to the company's operations while I was abroad, I had to empower the people I was leaving in the United States to act on my behalf. It was no small task. I talked to our bookkeeper and set out guidelines for the profit margins we needed to have, how revenue would be reported every month, and how cash flow would be reported every two weeks, so we could be sure we would make payroll on time.

In addition to the critical financial processes, I had scripts for sales-people and guidelines for handling clients' objections. I had checklists for how to start conversations and finish conversations. I had formats for every aspect of the work we did; I had systematized every company process and our financial model so that revenue could continue to be generated despite my absence.

Looking back at that experience now, from the perspective of someone who has helped many business owners scale, I'm grateful that I had read the right books, had the right mentors, and had the right instincts to have even the slightest idea of how to do this. The systematization came to me naturally, and that is what got me to the They Do It stage so quickly. By creating those processes, I empowered everyone in my business to have the same success, whether I was present or not. Everyone knew what his or her role was, and it was clear how we needed to work for everyone to win. Everyone had plenty of work to do and kept generating more revenue every day.

I had built a highly profitable, debt-free business that had stability without my day-to-day involvement. That is not to say that everything went completely smoothly and that there weren't growing pains. My systems were not quite bulletproof yet. I learned a lot from that process, and that has informed the roadmap I have created for you. In upcoming chapters, you will read about some of the tactics I honed after that experience that will serve you well, such as the Sticky Challenge, the 4Ps, and the 3Rs.

To employ a convenient metaphor, people often believe that once you magically scale to the top of a mountain, there is no possibility of getting knocked back down. But the reality is that each climb is hard, and every time you gather yourself together and head back up, the circumstances might be different. Yet what does not change are the tools you need to scale back up the mountain. These tools remain essentially the same, whatever the circumstances. And you will find them right on your 7-Figure Business Roadmap.

Now that we've gone through the three main stages on the roadmap, I want to reiterate the most important part of each level. In broad terms, they are the following:

1. I Do It: Focus on industry learning and growth.
2. We Do It: Focus on developing and sharing systems and processes for your business.
3. They Do It: Focus on hiring people and realizing your vision.

This is not to say that at each stage of the business you won't have to focus on client acquisition and people. The difference is in the level of challenge you add. To jump to the next level, meeting these challenges becomes paramount.

Scale Accelerator: MyOutdesk.com/7FigureRoadMap

Chapter 5

The 7-Figure Business Roadmap: How to Read It!

Now I introduce you to the six substages of growth—two for each level. Examining those will enable you to pinpoint more exactly where you are on the map. As you will see, each stage has characteristic revenue ranges, team sizes, challenges, and drivers associated with it.

Where Are You on the Roadmap?

The value in learning about these six substages is that they can help you look at the roadmap and say, "Yep, that was me last year," or, "That's my current problem exactly!" Then you will look ahead to the next stage up and say, "Yes, that is exactly where I want to go. I see what I need to do."

You may identify as being at a point somewhere in between two stages; for example, you might decide you have some aspects of substage three and some of substage four. If that happens, great! You can now identify the steps you need to take to plant yourself more firmly in substage four, while looking ahead to see how you can ultimately move beyond it. You may even realize as you study the substages that you have been pretending to be something that you are not. You may be pretending to be in substage four, meaning you are already in a substage-four mindset, but given your real day-to-day tasks and challenges, you are truly in substage three.

What lies at the heart of the process is identifying what your obstacles are because you will need to clear them to get to the next stage. Often, there are only one or two constraints that are keeping you from moving up the scale. It usually has to do with either some form of marketing, sales, leadership, or model.

You may also find that, at some point, you have leapfrogged a substage with your business, as I did with my real estate company. In that instance, I went from substage four to a substage six. You can leapfrog by having one huge new client, hiring somebody amazing who brings a lot of business with him or her, or acquiring another business. If you choose to do that, the roadmap will be able to help you by identifying all the potential steps you may have skipped that could lead to instability down the road.

You will have no doubt when you reach substage six because, at that point, you will be netting a million dollars!

At this point, you should go get some paper and start making notes, so you can place yourself and your business on the map. You can't follow the map forward until you find out what your starting point is, can you? First, determine the following:

1. How many employees do I have?
2. What is my annual revenue, and what was my net income (as reported on my schedule K-1) last year?

Those are your bottom-line factors. Use them to find out which substage you are in.

Roadmap Instructions

To help you follow these instructions, look ahead to the substage charts on the next few pages.

Once you have determined what substage you're starting at, note the challenges from the previous stage. Cross out those challenges you have already solved. If one or two remain, that's OK. Now you know about them, and you know you must address them before you can gain forward momentum.

Look next at the challenges for the substage you are in right now. Which ones make the most sense to you? If a challenge resonates with you and makes you think, "Yes, I am having this challenge right now," you know what problems you need to solve to move on to the next substage.

If you are a substage three Managing Leader, for example, and want to be a substage four Business Owner, hiring the right people and striking a life/work balance may be your biggest problems now. Write down three to five challenges you will have to conquer to emerge into the next substage of growth.

Now peek at the substage ahead of where you are now. You don't have to solve the challenges yet, but you should be aware of them. It's good to have a clear view of the road ahead as you begin to make decisions that will change your business.

Don't worry if you find that your business doesn't fit neatly into a single substage. You might be a substage five business in terms of revenue, but in terms of employee head count, you are a three. Conversely, you might have some of the challenges of a substage six Visionary Leader but be only at substage four in revenue and head count. That's OK. I have arranged the substages according to what data and our experience with over four thousand clients have told us. As long as you know exactly how you are bridging the categories and why, you will be able to identify your obstacles to growth and navigate a clear way forward.

Scale Accelerator: Throughout your journey on the 7-Figure Business Roadmap, client acquisition, lead generation, and people leadership will remain focal points for you. Why? Because they are the fuel that allows your business to scale. They always need a business owner's attention. Visit https://www.MyOutDesk.com/Accelerator.

Hang on to the information you have collected because we will refer to it in the upcoming chapters.

THE 7-FIGURE BUSINESS ROADMAP
▌I DO IT

Substage 1 MICROBUSINESS

New and existing business owners who are seeking consistency and growth and are committed to finding a better way and growing a successful, value-added business.

Total employees: Solo
Gross revenue: $0–60K

Challenges:
Money, Mindset, Market knowledge, Business knowledge, Account, Ability, Motivation, Sales skills, Roadmap, People skills

What it feels like: Adrift

How you know you've made it:
You have tapped in to your sphere of influence, established your expertise and knowledge of your business, and have the clarity and mindset necessary to be successful in your chosen business.

Core drives:
 - Mindset
 - Market knowledge

LEARN
An **"I Do It"** entrepreneur is new to an industry and has a hunger for learning and growth.

Figure 5.

THE 7-FIGURE BUSINESS ROADMAP
I DO IT

ENTREPRENEUR

Business owners who work solo in a business and are seeking a more rewarding career both financially and in quality of life.

Total Employees: Solo
Gross Revenue: $60–105K

Challenges:
Money, Mindset, Accountability, Strategic plan, Sales skills, People skills, Leads

What it feels like: Swamp

How you know you've made it:
You can articulate your differentiated value proposition to the marketplace to set appointments and win new business with ease and confidence.

Core drives:
 - People skills
 - Sales skills
 - Confidence

LEARN

An **"I Do It"** entrepreneur is new to an industry and has a hunger for learning and growth.

Figure 6.

THE 7-FIGURE BUSINESS ROADMAP
▌WE DO IT

Substage 3 MANAGING LEADER

Business professionals who are committed to doing the work required to establish their own independence and success.

Total employees: 1–2
Gross revenue: $105–330K

Challenges:
Consistency in revenue, Time management, Accountability, People/System leverage, Quality lead generation

What it feels like: Roller coaster

How you know you've made it:
You are constantly generating cash flow each month, have mastered dollar-productive activity, and are highly profitable.

Core drives:
  - Lead generation
  - Leverage

SYSTEM AND PROCESS

In the **"We Do It"** stage, your focus is to hire more people and create efficient systems and processes.

Figure 7.

THE 7-FIGURE BUSINESS ROADMAP
WE DO IT

Substage 4 BUSINESS OWNER

Business professionals who are committed to getting the most our of their choices to have an independent business by building a team and leveraging their time and money to get the greatest return for their efforts.

Total employees: 3–8
Gross revenue: $330K–1M

Challenges:
Hiring/Delegation; Attract, not chase; Marketing; Diversified; Revenue streams; Accountability; Building team; Life/Business balance

What it feels like: White Water

How you know you've made it:
Your business has shifted to attract, not chase, new clients, and you have at least five predictable revenue pillars in place in your business with key hires to manage those revenue-generating pillars.

Core drives:
- Systems
- Lead management
- Profitability

SYSTEM AND PROCESS

In the **"We Do It"** stage, your focus is to hire more people and create efficient systems and processes.

Figure 8.

THE 7-FIGURE BUSINESS ROADMAP
▌THEY DO IT

Substage 5 THE CEO

Driven business professionals who are committed to leading and building a permanent business that delivers value-added client experiences, provides long-term success, and increases their quality of life.

Total employees: 9–11
Gross revenue: $1–2.5M

Challenges:
Conquer the chaos, Systems, Processes, Hiring/People leadership, Life/Business balance, Building a client community, Company culture

What it feels like: Tornado

How you know you've made it:
You've built a business that has a clearly articulated vision; completely aligned core values among all team members; daily, weekly, and monthly accountability; and systems and processes in place to manage the client experience with or without your involvement.

Core drives:
- Strategy
- Leadership

WEALTH - WISDOM - PEOPLE - VISION
Once you hit the **"They Do It"** stage, the production of the business is no longer reliant on you. The company continues to sell and move forward with the systems in place.

Figure 9.

THE 7-FIGURE BUSINESS ROADMAP
THEY DO IT

Substage 6 VISIONARY

World-class professionals who have met their initial income and success goals, seeking to be challenged to improve in all areas of life while building an asset that provides wealth and prosperity for generations.

Total employees: 12+
Gross revenue: $2.5M+

Challenges:
Business model, Profitability, Leadership, Building a client community, Roles and responsibilities, Company vision, Company culture

What it feels like: Tar Pit

How you know you've made it:
You understand your financial model and have built a highly profitable debt-free business that generates profits for you without your involvement in day-to-day activities, and you are paid a salary from the profits your business generates.

Core drives:
- Vision
- Stability

WEALTH - WISDOM - PEOPLE - VISION

Once you hit the **"They Do It"** stage, the production of the business is no longer reliant on you. The company continues to sell and move forward with the systems in place.

Figure 10.

Chapter 6

Time and Talent Analysis: The Sticky Challenge

You have discovered where you and your business are on the 7-Figure Business Roadmap and have identified three to five challenges you will need to overcome to scale your business. Now we are going to do a simple but effective exercise to determine how you and your employees are spending your time.

Wealthy people become so because they understand leverage.

There are 3,600 seconds in an hour, and 28,800 seconds in a full eight-hour workday. As *Rich Dad, Poor Dad* author Robert Kiyosaki has pointed out, wealthy people become so because they understand leverage. And one of the things you can leverage is time. The practice you are about to undertake will determine the leverage you have with your day-to-day activities.

If you were to go to a doctor, the doctor's first step would be to find a diagnosis. This exercise is a kind of diagnostic tool for your business; it will help you evaluate what you and your team, however large or small it is, are focused on. It will help you break down what your day looks like and will enable you to see where you can buy back some time. I call this time-freedom the temporal space you need to strategize and think.

Many of our clients are surprised when they see the results of this exercise. Using leverage correctly is a tricky skill, and some people never master it. A common stumbling block is that there are tasks you want done in a particular way—what you think of as the "right way." However, this mindset is dangerous because there isn't enough time in the day to truly have a hand in everything. The key is to do only the tasks that will impact your business goals.

I call the following exercise The Sticky Challenge. It is easy to undertake; you and/or your company can use this tool to do a full leverage inventory in just one week.

The concept is simple: You will record every single one of your actions on a separate sticky note throughout the day. You might write, "I made a phone call to a client," "I grabbed some food," or "I had a sales meeting," one per sticky. At the end of the investigation period, you will sit down and categorize your activities into three different areas:

1. Dollar-productive activities
2. Non-dollar-productive activities
3. Legacy vs. non-legacy activities

The concept of what is dollar productive is fairly obvious. Legacy vs. non-legacy might strike you as a subtler distinction. Figure 11 offers an example to help explain the terms.

$ PRODUCTIVE ACTIVITIES	NON $ PRODUCTIVE ACTIVITIES	
• Networking events • Sales presentations • Negotiating with clients and vendors • Prospecting for new clients • Work your yeferral network	• Building out a talent management system • Building a referral program • Building out CRM • Creating standards and procedures	LEGACY
	• Meeting prep • Administrative tasks • Payroll • Running and monitoring the legacy programs	NON-LEGACY

Figure 11.

A legacy task is anything that gives you leverage inside your business; the setting up of a legacy task, like building out a CRM or a referral program, is the ultimate gift because it creates time-freedom. Non-legacy tasks are more routine with a short-lived impact.

Codie decides to try the Sticky Challenge.

Real-Life Success Story: Codie's Sticky Challenge Experience

My good friend Codie came to a point in her business when she wanted a new road to travel down. She was putting in up to eighty hours a week, every week (when we did an analysis together, the average was seventy-seven). Although her business was doing well, she was exhausted. I suggested that Codie begin with seeing if she could earn some time-freedom by doing the Sticky Challenge. She said, "Okay, Daniel, you're a little crazy, but I'll see what happens."

Here is how to complete the Sticky Challenge. Grab a stack of sticky notes and follow yourself around for a whole week, writing down everything you do. If you can do two to four weeks, that's even better. After compiling a list of all of the tasks you do on a daily basis, the time it takes to complete, and the category ($ Productive, Non $ Productive, Legacy, Non-Legacy), then you can begin to get an idea of how you are spending your time at work. The magic of this simple yet effective "time on task" study is that your whole team can do it. You can then easily begin to prioritize the most important work ($ Productive) with the idea that, because you now have the data, you and your team can come up with ways to increase the value brought to the business.

Codie accepted the challenge, and what a revelation she had. She couldn't believe how much of her day was spent on non-dollar-productive and non-legacy activities. This was what one of her daily sticky arrays looked like:

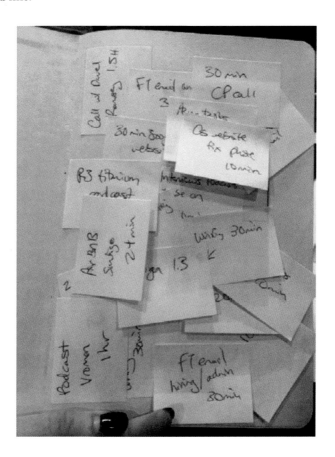

Scale Framework: Use the downloadable quick guide to The Sticky Challenge as an easy way to discover your company's leverage framework:

https://www.MyOutDesk.com/StickyChallenge

Codie realized that although she was having financial success and she had hired some people to work for her, she wasn't feeling productive. I liked the insights Codie was having at this point, but I told her she should do the challenge for another week to get an even better picture.

After two weeks, Codie had created complete metrics surrounding her workdays. Her conclusion was that only 37 percent of her days was spent on dollar-productive activities. Most of the time, she was just doing "stuff." And there was more as well; she was expending a lot of time and energy locked in mitigating a poor relationship with one of her coworkers. She was having a hard time focusing on all the great successes she'd had in her business—because of a power struggle with just one person. We helped her fix that relationship right away. They kept working together and had a better understanding of what their relationship should look like. More than that, this put Codie into a good mental space and clarified her big picture.

It is worth mentioning that Codie is a very successful and supersmart businesswoman. In terms of revenue and employees, she had the challenges of a substage five entrepreneur trying to move to a substage six. And yet, in terms of her daily work patterns, she was more of a substage three. She found herself doing remedial tasks, for example, marketing tasks. As entrepreneurs sometimes do, she was stuck in a mode of execution. She was spending so much time on non-legacy activities that it was time for her to step back and ask, "What are the most important things in my day? Whom can I hire so that I can focus on my dollar-productive and legacy activities?"

With the information we gathered from the Sticky Challenge, we were able to answer those questions. She subsequently hired several people, so she could stop doing the more low-level sales. We also needed to restructure her team and reorganize their responsibilities. Though she would have to spend some money and time in the hiring process, we knew (from experience) that she would see a quick enough increase in sales and profits to make it more than worthwhile.

Wise Effort

In today's business world, we like to think that our strategies are all fresh and new, but the truth is many illustrious historical figures performed the same kinds of time analyses like the Sticky Challenge. Founding father Thomas Jefferson's daily calendar, for example, is fascinating. He had affirmations in the morning and time for thinking; he journaled and organized tasks in a "what I need to do to succeed" list. Success for Jefferson was not just getting a lot of things done, and it shouldn't be for you either. Success is crossing the finish line of a business outcome you are striving for or buying back more time or making more of an impact on the world. You will find that putting a leverage framework around your day is massively empowering.

The Sticky Challenge was the brainchild of a client of ours, Lisa Archer. Lisa runs twelve offices across the country, and since she isn't sitting in an office with her direct reports most of the time, she isn't able to spend a lot of time with them. She came up with this method to help everyone realize what they are up to, in order to give them opportunities to see how they can provide maximum value. It was so effective that we adopted it too.

To those around me, I seem like a natural at finding the best possible use of my time, but I wasn't always that way. Luckily, my grandma was a good model for me. One day, I asked her if she could bring me along with her on her job cleaning houses, so I could see how she made money. I was nine, so she wasn't keen on bringing me, but she indulged me. I was curious but clueless, and she chose to enlighten me. There were worse things I could have been doing.

When we arrived at Grandma's first client's house, she gave me a broom and told me to clean the garage. Then she left to clean the inside. I looked around, and I saw what I deemed a disaster: sawdust, oil, boxes, spiders, and bicycle parts. The concrete was cracked, and there was even something funky on the walls. I knew I would have to wipe those walls down. So, I did what I thought I should. I started in one five-by-five corner, and over the course of an hour, I cleaned it perfectly.

When Grandma came back, she said, "What are you doing?" "I'm cleaning the garage like you said," I answered. A resigned sigh escaped her. She grabbed a broom, and in less than five minutes, she swept the entire garage, went and got the trash can, threw it on the ground, and swept in all the debris. She ripped up all the boxes, shoved everything she could into that trash can, and set it by the curb. Then she looked up and said, "What have you been doing for the last hour?"

Grandma was the first person to teach me all about what my wife calls "wise effort." We all need a plan around managing our days at work, and until you stop to analyze what you are doing, you will never be able to make one. What the Sticky Challenge does is to get you out of the corner of the garage and looking at the big picture, spiders and all.

Drill Down to Your Unique Skill Set

As you do this challenge, think about how your daily activities relate to what your superpowers are. Ask yourself, "What am I uniquely skilled at doing?" Ideally, your organization will include people with a variety of talents, and you will be mostly doing what you are best at. There are a lot of business books on the market these days about how finding your unique talents and homing in on them is a practice that garners success. You should take them seriously. If you have the right systems within your business, you can work toward spending 70 or 80 percent of your time doing the things that you are uniquely skilled to do. Everything else gets leveraged away.

Every business needs a talent-management system that, once inputted, creates predictable results. It might include a sales system, a marketing system, a human resources system, and even a system for ordering snacks and coffee for the breakroom. Once all these systems are in place, they give you leverage. One of the reasons everyone loves Amazon is because there is leverage in the Amazon system. When you buy on Amazon, you don't have to go to a store. You don't have to spend much time on the site, and you don't even have to get out your credit card. You click one button, and the thing you want shows up the next day. That is a highly effective system. If you create highly effective systems in your business, you are as likely to succeed at a higher level than your competitors because such systems enable growth.

Creating a system inside your business is a legacy task: It is non-dollar-productive in the short-term, but it is beneficial in terms of future potential. You may want to hire someone to do this piece for you. Your reservation will likely be that you can't afford to hire someone to do these things because you aren't making the revenue to pay them. The flip side of that is that if you start spending more time focusing on your dollar-productive activities, you will produce those dollars. It can be a difficult mental leap to make, especially for those in the early and middle stages of the roadmap. I know many people, business veterans, who have chosen to start businesses without ever doing any of the legacy or non-legacy tasks. These are people who already understand leverage and the concept of staying within your strength zone. They are happy to delegate that entire side of the business. There is no one pattern that fits all businesses, but having an awareness of what categories your activities fall in, within the context of your talent areas, will breed success.

Many people can't let go of the non-dollar-productive side of their business because they are stuck in the "I want it done my way" mindset. After you complete the Sticky Challenge, I guarantee that won't be you. Instead, you will be taking the first step toward becoming laser-focused on what will make your business grow.

Scale Accelerator: Take your previous year's federal tax filings, look at your adjusted gross income, and divide that by fifty-two. Then divide that by your average hourly work week. This number represents the baseline hourly rate of financial value you create for yourself.

Figure 12. Visit https://www.MyOutDesk.com/Accelerator.

In summary, devote a week (or several weeks) to the Sticky Challenge, making an inventory of your activities and charting them into categories. This will give you a clear picture of what you are putting your energy and talents into. Review your hourly rate and then reflect on whom you can hire to give you the time-freedom that you need to scale.

Chapter 7

Why Virtual Professionals?

Iris, one of MyOutDesk's VPs, sent me this picture from the hospital:

She was in the hospital with her husband, working. Iris is so dedicated to her job and responsible that she simply didn't want to let her client down. Another time, a flood hit the town of another one of our virtual professionals, Tai (pronounced like "bow tie"). As the water invaded her house, she settled her beautiful baby daughter on her hip, grabbed some food and her laptop, and moved upstairs, a floor at a time, so she could continue working. When she made it to the roof, she was still at it. "Are you nuts, Tai?" I asked over email. "You should probably get out of there!"

"I still have an internet connection," she said with cool confidence. "I have a chair up here. Besides, the weather is fine."

I had to laugh. "But why did you stay in the house?" I asked.

"I had client work to do," she replied, as if I were Captain Oblivious. Both of those stories are simply pure motivation.

If there is one thing I want you to take away from this chapter, it is that there are so many people around the world who are talented and hungry to work hard to provide value for their clients. When I describe how to scale your business with virtual professionals, it is best for you to understand that I am not suggesting merely farming out remedial tasks for low hourly wages. I am suggesting leveraging high-quality, global talent.

In fact, MyOutDesk has always preferred the term "virtual professionals" to "virtual assistants." When I hired my first VP, in 2007, I was like most Americans: I had no idea how advanced and motivated people were. Back then, I owned a couple of different businesses, and over the subsequent ten years, I learned all that virtual professionals can do for a business from a talent and motivation perspective. I have also learned how rewarding it is to provide hope and opportunity to as many people as possible throughout the world by giving them wages and benefits that reflect their true value.

The American Dream on a Global Scale

Our virtual professionals have a drive to succeed in the new global economy in the same way that American immigrants have always valued fresh opportunities by physically coming to the United States. These people are highly motivated to improve their quality of life, and we simply give them an opportunity to help our clients scale their businesses. In return, they give our company high-quality work and their priceless energy and loyalty. What we do is take the American Dream and export it. Our virtual professionals hitch their wagons to ours, so to speak.

A Day in the Life of a MyOutDesk Virtual Professional

For the first several years of my career, I was heavily United States–based and simply augmenting my operations with virtual professionals in the

Philippines. But after coming to understand who these folks really are and what they can do (and after the epiphany I had on my honeymoon about my own need to truly delegate), I went all in. I decided virtual professionals would become a massive part of my businesses, and that decision has paid off exponentially. It really did give me more freedom to live my life while helping me build businesses worth owning.

I believe there are ten qualities that demonstrate that a person, wherever he or she might live, is a super talent and, therefore, hirable to help you scale:

1. Punctuality
2. Work ethic
3. Effort
4. Body language
5. Energy
6. Passion
7. Coachability
8. Doing extra
9. Being prepared
10. Attitude

Our virtual professionals have these qualities in abundance. The appeal of employing them goes far beyond just buying the same level of work for a quarter or a third of what it would cost domestically; it is a joy to see them bring these ten qualities to work with them every day. And what's more, their ethic has been infectious and inspiring for our US team members. When our team at home hears stories like Tai's, it really puts things in perspective.

How is this all possible, you ask? Technology is what makes all our collaborations with virtual professionals practicable. There is no office our employees report to in the Philippines; everyone works from home while logged on to a server or a technology platform that tracks employee hours and all the work they do. As MyOutDesk has grown, we have spent millions ensuring our work platform is state-of-the-art.

This is a common sight in the Philippines.

Working this way is appealing to people in the Philippines for many compelling reasons. The first is that it has given our professionals the ability to avoid traffic. We all hate to commute and like to reduce our time on the road whenever possible, but traffic in the Philippines is out-of-this-world terrible. It compares to no stateside, rush-hour traffic pattern that you might be familiar with. Because the Philippines has 1950s road infrastructure with a 2020 population, the typical commute into the office is about two hours. Two agonizing hours. Once at the office, employees generally work a ten-hour day and drive two hours home again.

I'm sure you can easily see why people in the Philippines would be excited to work for us from home. We buy them back a lot of their time—and maybe even their sanity—which is a great value proposition for them.

Another reason they are so highly motivated to work for US clients from home is that it allows parents to stay with their children. Typically, parents who work for us will log in when their kids go to bed, which aligns their workday with US time zones. When the kids wake up, their workday is done. They can take the kids to school and then sleep during the school day. When the kids come home at three or four in the afternoon, the family has the whole evening ahead of them. Parents can make dinner, help with the kids' studies, and play. This is a luxury that many parents in the Philippines do not have.

Working from home gives parents who would otherwise barely get to see their children make a quantum leap in terms of quality of life, and they repay us for this in spades with the quality of their work.

There are still more ways we can elevate the standard of living of our virtual professionals in the Philippines. Many of the social safety nets we are accustomed to in countries like the United States, such as retirement funds, insurance, and the stock market, are largely unavailable to them in their economy. Parents work to provide for their children, and when the parents grow old, it flip-flops: children take care of their parents in return. They don't have our retirement model. We help by being the only online job company that provides health-care insurance to its VPs and their spouses as well as to children and aging parents as well. Socioeconomically, this is a huge advantage for them and really helps them save their money for better things. We provide this while paying our virtual professionals 40 percent more than any other online job company and providing annual raises, vacation time, and short-term microloans for business equipment and school for their children. In sum, we give our virtual professionals the rewards and benefits they would have if they were working for us here in the United States. We even have two conferences a year and an annual Christmas party in the Philippines. We are fully invested in our mutual happiness and success.

Busting the Big Myth: The English Language in the Philippines

It is worth underscoring the fact that English is taught in schools in the Philippines from a very young age. The Philippine archipelago consists of more than seven thousand islands, and more than five thousand of those are inhabited. Naturally, multiple dialects evolved that mirror the topographical separations among the scattered towns that make up the country. There are 182 living dialects in the Philippines. That is why English has become, as a matter of convenience, the one language that connects everyone in the Philippines. That is the language street signs are written in, medical journals are written in, and laws are written in. English has overcome the barriers posed by having numerous dialects and has allowed the Philippines to better participate in the global market. As such, anyone who has an education, owns a car, or owns a home is almost guaranteed to be highly proficient in speaking and writing English.

It is also worth mentioning that, culturally, people from the Philippines tend to be very much aligned with people in America. Because the Spanish colonized it in the sixteenth century, the vast majority (93 percent) of people self-identify as Catholic and keep many of the traditions, holidays, and general values surrounding business as people in the West do.

The Bottom Line: It's a Win-Win Partnership

I have found that there are many positives about working with our virtual professionals:

1. Time zones are not a barrier.
2. Culture is not a barrier.
3. Language is not a barrier.
4. The principle of currency arbitrage means money is also not a barrier.

I am taking care to establish the multitude of positive qualities that properly vetted virtual professionals can bring to your company not because I ever doubted the superpowers of these talented, intelligent people but because you might. There are a lot of companies out there who simply arrange for cheap labor for mundane tasks, but that is not what I am suggesting you do to scale your business. My secret to success has been that I have seized an opportunity created by an alignment of interests between businesses in the United States and professionals in the Philippines and elsewhere in the world.

In the chapters that follow, I focus on the growth this alignment can bring to your business. As you learn how to leverage virtual professionals, remember that hiring them also brings hope and opportunity that impact their home too.

The MyOutDesk Origin Story: Lily

One of the stories that I love to share any time I have the opportunity is the story of how MyOutDesk began with a single, wonderful professional. When I was in real estate and recovering from the global financial crisis, my brother introduced me (virtually) to Lily, who had been doing some work for him from the Philippines through a freelancing website. He had chosen her from over two hundred applicants.

She had been doing a little assistant work for me as well, for a short while, when I mentioned in passing that I was spearheading some rebranding of the business and had paid a designer $1,000 to create a logo and some business cards for me. In that recovery phase of my business, $1,000 seemed like a lot of money—yet another expense in a list of many—and I hadn't even liked what they had produced for me so far. I was down about it. Lily told me she would try to create a better logo for me for free. Why? Because she wanted to show me the level of work she was capable of. She wasn't convinced that I understood just how talented she was, and she was right. I was very happy with the result. We ended up using her logo instead of the designer's.

Lily saw an opportunity working virtually for a US business. At the time she began working for my brother, she had two small children, one of them an infant, and she was working at a call center. To make the long commutes to her job, she had been surviving on just four hours of sleep on workdays and didn't feel like she had enough time or energy for her family.

Since the quality of her work was so outstanding, I asked her if she could find more people like her who could do quality work like her. We would employ them through an entirely new company called MyOutDesk. Without strategically planning it, she became the de facto leader of MOD in the Philippines. Lily became a star recruiter for MyOutDesk. Working virtually had been a boon for her and her family, and she wanted others in her area to have the same freedom and prosperity.

Back then, few people were working with virtual employees, but our business helping others hire faraway employees took off quickly. Our first client went from five to seventeen VPs with a completely revamped organizational model in short order, and he told me, "Daniel, our virtual professionals have shaved $250,000 off our monthly overhead." He was able to reinvest that money in the business and see supercharged growth. Around the same time, we had our first MODCon convention in the Philippines, and that was when I truly came to understand what Lily already knew: There was an enormous talent base in the Philippines, and I had tapped into something quite powerful. That visit was a profound experience because, as an American, I had not fully grasped the quality of global talent until I saw it with my own eyes.

With teams on both sides of the ocean, we were able to help more and more clients scale their businesses, and scale MyOutDesk exponentially at the same time. We thought we had reached a huge milestone in 2012 with one hundred virtual professionals, but little did we know that we would grow to have ten times that number, as we do today. Lily has said, "I think when you came to visit that first time, you saw that these people you had employed were not just names. They were people with families that you have a big impact on. Looking back, what makes me filled with joy is knowing that there are thousands of families here in the Philippines who are living well because we have MyOutDesk."

Lily is a great at explaining to clients exactly what makes our blended work model a success. She tells new clients, "We're here to make your life easy. Things that you can't do while you're out of the office, we're here to do for you. This is going to give you more time to focus on what drives your revenue rather than being tied up doing tasks."

Lily's path in life has not always been easy, and she enjoys that we have an opportunity to pay it forward in the Philippines. Always one to see the value in philanthropy, she is one of the team's most enthusiastic supporters of our charitable organization: MOD Movement. One of the organizations we have been able to help there is Boystown, an orphanage near the resort where we have our conferences. Lily visited Boystown and immediately felt we could help. Since then, the MyOutDesk team has gone back time and again because, as Lily pointed out, "Those children are never without a need. These are abandoned kids, hungry kids. We have donated food and clothing, and have even done repairs to their Foundling House, which houses infants and toddlers. These babies were living in a tough spot, and our virtual professionals were happy to take the time to completely rehab their home and do anything else they could that was needed." She quickly explained why: "Because we feel we are blessed in so many ways."

Visit https://MODMovement.org to see the charity work our clients and our company have completed since 2013.

Chapter 8

Outcomes: How to Restructure to Scale

Now that you have a good idea of which activities you need to delegate in order to scale your business, you are probably beginning to build a picture of the VPs you will need and what you see them doing for you. Before you start to go down that road, however, let's take a moment to make a simple but important distinction between tasks and outcomes. In the old industrial economy, people went to work and performed a job based on a job description. They could go to work with a list of tasks in mind, tick them off, and clock out at the end of the day. If they accomplished the tasks that fell within their area of responsibility, they got paid and continued to have a job the next day. Many jobs are still defined that way today.

Yet in our postindustrialized, global economy, clinging to task-based thinking is at best inefficient and, at worst, a significant disadvantage. Task-based thinking and getting stuck in the day-to-day grind of your business are closely related; they both keep you from taking advantage of the exponential growth potential that a connected world full of technological wonders and automated systems presents us.

At MyOutDesk, we don't suggest you hire VPs to perform tasks. We suggest you hire people who will meet your outcomes. Tasks are activities or objectives with no measurable end goals; all that is required to turn a task into a desired outcome is some reflection and clarity.

Let's say, for example, you have hired a sales assistant in your real estate business. One of your hopes in hiring this person is that he will be able to use his time to get more referrals from current clients for your business.

Thus, you have tasked your new employee with calling all your clients. Once you have revenue from this employee's efforts, it will easily justify the expense of hiring him. Correct? Well, not always. If you give the employee a job description and tell him to call your clients, he may come back to you later and say, "OK, I did that." When you don't see any new referrals and point that out, the employee could say, "But I did the job, just like you said. I did exactly what you told me to do."

"I wanted you to call our clients," you explain, "but you were supposed to get more referrals. In fact, I wanted to have at least 10 percent of our clients refer us business. Did you ask the clients for a referral?"

"I didn't know you wanted me to do that," says the employee.

This is the problem with job descriptions that don't focus on an outcome. What would be far more empowering for the employee in this case is knowing a desired outcome to meet for the business: a clearly defined, measurable end state to help everyone understand what the job is and why it needs to be done. That kind of clarity can easily be wrapped into an outcome statement.

I have found that outcome statements are more motivating and more effective not only for business owners but for employees as well. A good outcome statement for this scenario would be:

"Your job is to get 10 percent of our current and/or previous clients to refer business to us."

When you describe areas of responsibility with an end-state methodology, what you are doing is setting everyone up to win. You have a mutual understanding around the delivery of that outcome and look at the process of achieving it with a degree of vision. A mere task is transformed into an intention that is measurable.

To give another example, let's say you want to increase your business by 10 percent in the next year, so you hire a new salesperson. Rather than telling the new employee her job is to "do sales," give her an outcome statement:

"Your job is to generate and handle 10 percent more sales compared to last year."

That statement provides clarity and a measurable outcome. That way, she will know that if she increases revenue to the 5 percent mark, it is time to identify what it will take to get to the next level. She can immediately understand what it will take to sustain her salary and make her efforts valuable to the business. Moreover, this statement includes a metric so that any progress can be periodically measured.

An important concept that goes hand in hand with the shift to outcome-based thinking is making the mental shift away from "How Pies" and toward "Who Pies." Business owners stuck in the How Pie way of thinking tend to see a job that needs doing and default to "How can I get this done?" This will almost inevitably result in your doing more work, which, in turn, keeps you stuck on the 7-Figure Business Roadmap. Instead, step into the Who Pie: Ask, "Whom can I hire to get this done?" We have found that being able to release the how and focus on who is what allows businesses to grow. Here is an example using an outcome that any business might have:

Define Your Desired Outcomes

Every business should spend time to develop outcomes that include a metric signaling when the outcome has been achieved. The activities of your virtual professionals and your employees at home should always be tied to the core business outcomes. There are only five core outcomes that you should hire talent for:

1. Enhancing the customer experience
2. Growing the business
3. Lowering costs
4. Increasing productivity
5. Improving quality

Once you arrive at an outcome, we apply a handy formula to it to help you conceptualize its having been accomplished. There are four aspects to this formula.

1. Direction: Are you increasing or decreasing the matrix?
2. Object of control: What facet of your business will you be measuring?
3. Unit of measurement: Will you be measuring change by percentages, raw numbers, or another measure?
4. Contextual clarifier: What is the condition under which the measure is relevant?

The business owners we coach find that charting outcomes in this clearly defined, visual way, as seen in figure 13, is exceptionally helpful.

Direction	Object of Control	Unit of Measure	Contextual Clarifier
Decrease the cost	of my financial reporting	by 15% from previous year	using a MyOutDesk Accounting Virtual Professional

Figure 13.

Real-Life Success Story: Becoming More Efficient with Ultimate Autographs

Ultimate Autographs is a national sports memorabilia company. It is in sub-stage five on the roadmap and is co-owned by Dave Sollis and his brother. When Dave came to us, one of his challenges was getting through a backlog of thirty or forty designs that needed to get done so they could put them on apparel, gear, and other products they sell. Ultimate Autographs had experienced a lot of missed opportunities in terms of expanding their product line to meet the market quickly, and all of it could be traced back to their inefficient design process. At the time, they were using a third-party designer that was taking five to seven days to complete each design they submitted. What's more, each time they requested changes to a design, it would take another day or two to finalize. It was extremely frustrating for Dave.

I use the example of Ultimate Autographs because the constraint Dave had was so easily identifiable: He needed graphics design to come in-house so his company could get designs done faster. The product-design development speed was just not sufficient to get the company to substage six and netting a million dollars. The outcome framework we came up with looked like figure 14:

Direction	Object of Control	Unit of Measure	Contextual Clarifier	Optional Example
Increase the number of hours	on product and graphic design	to eight hours per day (full-time)	to increase online sales and direct sales	of the sport mystery box (their primary product)

Figure 14.

One day after I coached Dave through this new outcome, I got this text message from him:

> Daniel, don't want to bother you with a phone call but I have to say thank you. The experience has been great so far, and we have finalized a virtual professional today after interviewing 4. Super impressed so far.

Do you know what happened to Ultimate Autographs after making this simple change of hiring a design professional? Each design that once took more than a week to finalize now takes a couple of hours. The company has doubled its revenue and is on the way to scaling. It is a great example of the raw power a virtual professional can bring to a small business. Every business has constraints to get to the next level, and if you have gone through the experience of removing one, you know that it is transformative. It is like playing basketball—perhaps you are only able to do layups at first. Then you decide to go to the free-throw line and shoot there, but you miss a lot. But you keep at it, and you get better and find you can make a basket from the next line back. Soon, you are making half-court shots! Those are the shots we want you to be able to make by identifying your outcomes and solving for them.

The Priority Matrix

As you take on your outcomes, it is important to run them through a "priority matrix." This is a concept invented by President Eisenhower and popularized by Steven Covey in *The 7 Habits of Highly Effective People*. We have designed our own matrix specifically to quantify the effort your outcomes will require for you to achieve them and the impact that each priority would have on your business. You should place each outcome you develop into one of four quadrants. (See figure 15.)

The diagram makes the process self-explanatory: If an outcome requires little effort and has a big impact, it should be your number one priority. Conversely, if an outcome requires a lot of effort but will only move the needle in your business slightly, it should be low on your list, or even struck off it. The maybes that fall into the middle range could be lower on your priority list, or perhaps this is your signal to delegate them to someone else.

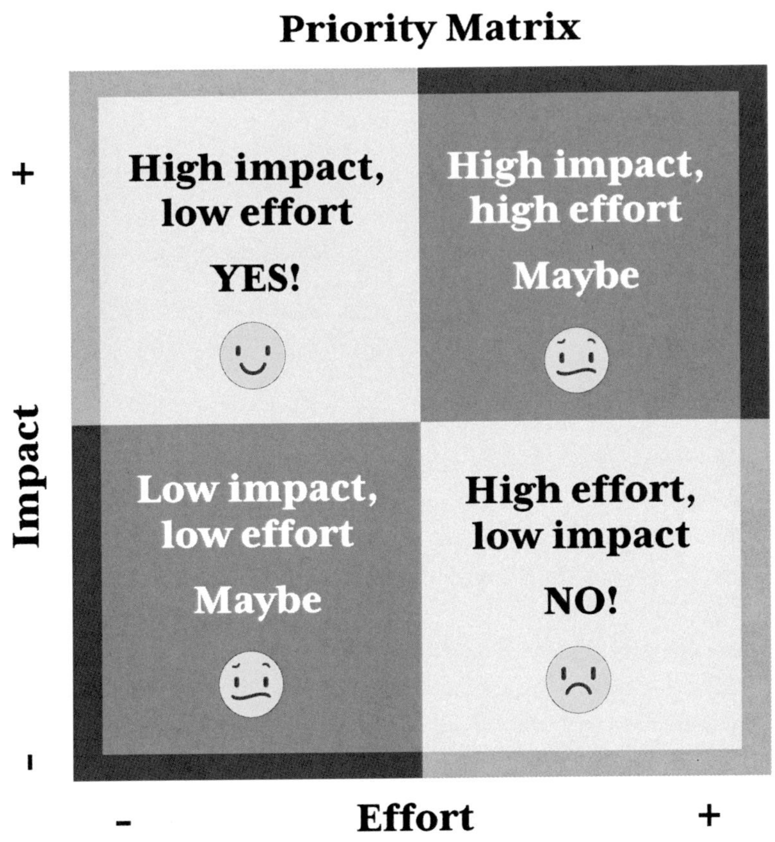

Priority Matrix

	High impact, low effort YES! 🙂	High impact, high effort Maybe 😐
Impact	Low impact, low effort Maybe 😐	High effort, low impact NO! 🙁

−   Effort   +

Figure 15.

Once you have an outcome, you need to figure out who will be the right person to work to complete that outcome. This might be someone already on your team, or it might be someone you need to hire or outsource to. You might put an outcome in the priority matrix and think, "Gosh, this is a high priority, and right now there's nobody on the team who could do this because everyone's capacity is just gone." If that is the case, to make this outcome happen, you'll need to find someone new. Perhaps a VP would be a good fit for this slice of Who Pie.

Real-Life Success Story: David Greene and the Priority Matrix

David Greene is a friend, bestselling author, public speaker, and all-around amazing guy. I identify with him because he comes from a humble upbringing just like I do. David started his career as a cop and was one for nine years. In 2015, David and I drove up to the Yosemite Valley and stayed in a cabin with my business peer group. That one weekend in a cabin completely transformed his life: He took a leave of absence from the police force and started a career as a professional speaker, trainer, coach, and real estate investor.

In his first year in business, he doubled his net worth, halved his working time, and began to have a life worth living. Following up with David after his first year in business was such a pleasure for me because he had listened to my advice, taken it, and crushed his personal goals. In early 2018, we reviewed all the projects he'd been working on. I introduced David to the idea of outcomes and the priority matrix.

David became a bestselling author by doing what all successful entrepreneurs do: find someone to add value to and then pour his heart and soul into adding value to that person. David's biggest concern was knowing what to focus his attention on next. He has so much on his plate and so many opportunities flying his way.

Scale Accelerator: Go to https://www.MyOutDesk.com /Outcomes to download an outcomes spreadsheet and instructions on how to execute it.

The priority matrix is an excellent tool for making strategic decisions around what outcomes you should pursue. We all have a finite amount of time available in this world; choosing what to focus on and what to say no to is always a challenge. David had an opportunity to help people as a coach, yet it would take a lot of work to set up a training platform, create a website, schedule weekly coaching calls, and develop a curriculum. He thought that because he was a coach at heart this would be the most fulfilling job he could do, but according to the priority matrix, this was a high-effort endeavor without the guarantee of high impact on his business.

David intuitively knew that he was doing a lot of work without prioritizing any of it in any specific order. I started asking him what things would involve a lower effort for him. What could he do without getting drained? These things would enhance his biggest opportunities and drive the value in what he was building. Because he was already a bestselling author and had already been approached for his second book, David knew that the highest-impact, lowest-effort (YES) activity he could undertake would be to write his second book. David's situation is a prime example of how to use our outcome framework, layered on top of the priority matrix, to define and create strategic initiatives for the calendar year. When you focus on the end goal like David did and complete the outcomes in the YES quadrant of the priority matrix first, your business will begin to scale while you maintain a good quality of life.

Chapter 9

The Revenue Model for Virtual Professionals: The 4Ps

Most business owners, as we have discussed, don't automatically have much clarity around what precisely their job is as an owner. You have probably identified some daily tasks through your Sticky Challenge that are non-dollar-productive. They might be paperwork-related, like accounting, or customer-related, like follow-up calls. No doubt, by now, you understand why you shouldn't be doing them. So, what should you be doing?

The answer is straightforward, if big: Your job is to create predictable revenue and scale your business. It is also to ensure that everything your employees are doing leads toward that overarching outcome. Why? Because revenue growth cures all problems. At some level, every company is in the business of selling, and to scale your business, your company will need to do it with ever-increasing efficiency.

The problem is that many business owners hit their stride when they become successful at selling, so their natural response to growing their business is to sell more and sell harder. It wasn't until I first started hiring salespeople that I began to realize that being a great salesperson was not where my true value was. My value was in having the vision and creating systems to generate more revenue and scale my business. I discovered that by delegating to my virtual professionals, I was able to remove virtually all my non-dollar-productive activities from my plate and the plates of my US employees, so we could focus on just those two things.

In every major corporation, the CEO, owner, or principals are focused on growing the company. These individuals are typically compensated with a bonus or salary structure that is tied to the percentages of growth they engender. There is good reason for this: When our companies are growing, our clients are served at the highest level possible, and we have the best available pool of talent. We have the best available technology and have profits to invest in infrastructure and training. Simply put, companies that are growing are alive. The flip side of that is that companies that are not growing are dying. That sounds extreme, but it is true. If I tell you your company is not growing as it should, you may object and say, "But look! We grew 5 percent last year." Now, 5 percent is a great number for a huge business, but for most midsize and small business, 5 percent isn't enough to enable you to do the things you want in life. That is the magic of delegating non-dollar-productive activities and focusing most of your company's activities on revenue generation.

Accenture's Sage but Expensive Advice for IBM

One of the best examples I can give you of a company that saved itself by making this realization is IBM. In the 1990s, IBM had flatlined. It had a revolving door of CEOs, and much of the board had been dismissed. The stock was plummeting as the company struggled to remain relevant. IBM's leaders knew that they had to do something new or face corporate death. They hired the management consultancy firm Accenture. For six months, Accenture interviewed support staff, salespeople, managers, and leaders. The team analyzed the company's activities much like you did yours with the Sticky Challenge and came up with one major conclusion: IBM needed to hire assistants for its sales team.

What had happened was that someone who ran IBM had a financial background rather than sales. Being a financial type, this person had inundated the sales team with documentation and contractual requirements. This meant that there was a mammoth amount of administrative and project-management work involved in closing deals. When Accenture did its inventory of the sales team's activities, it revealed that each salesperson was spending between 60 and 70 percent of work time on paperwork. They had very little time left to sell.

The solution to this problem probably seems like common sense to you, given all that you now know about dollar-productive activities. Yet even a company as big as IBM fell victim to the non-dollar-productive time suck, and what's more, they paid Accenture a million dollars for pointing it out. Being a nice guy, I've saved you those millions of dollars by pointing it out to you now.

The 4Ps

To help you maintain your focus on generating revenue, I will introduce you to the 4Ps. (See figure 16.) Everyone at MyOutDesk focuses on the 4Ps. When I left the country for six months in 2011, I set a goal of increasing our revenue using them. Not only did we double that goal using this system but we also ended up helping thousands of people find jobs with growing businesses across the United States. The 4Ps stand for Prospecting, Presenting, Persistent Follow-up, and Potential Referrals.

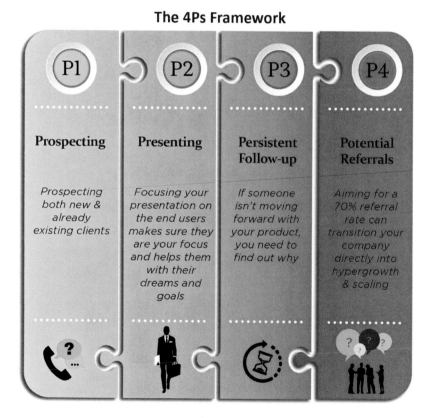

Figure 16.

Prospecting

Everyone understands what prospecting is, but not everyone understands how to measure it or how it drives revenue. At its most effective, prospecting isn't just going out to get new business from people you don't know. The reality is that you should be spending more time communicating with your existing clients to encourage them buy more from you or to earn referrals from them.

Sometimes the best thing to do is to simply call the clients currently in your sphere and say hello. What stops you from doing that? If you aren't already prospecting this way, it is probably because you don't want to sound like a sleazy salesperson and/or you wouldn't know what to say. You want people to like you. That is something many salespeople fear. The truth is that there are very simple ways to get through your resistance to prospecting existing clients. You can ask them what they accomplished in the past year and what their goals are for the coming year. It doesn't have to be a weird conversation along the lines of "I'm calling to see if you want to buy more insurance," or, "Call me if you want to buy a stock." It can simply be connecting to see if you can help them accomplish their hopes and dreams.

You can also touch base with something as simple as forwarding an article about something you know they are interested in. It shows them that you care about them and would like to be their partner in what they want to achieve in the world. That is one of the most important things you can do to drive more referrals. If you are not generating 70 percent of your business from referrals, I believe you have some work to do. That will require you to prospect not just every day but in the right way to get you to that 70 percent, so you can create a saleable business.

Another area you should be prospecting from is potential or high-probability clients. The best time to get a new client is when the client's life has shifted in some way. If you are an insurance broker, for example, who offers home, auto, and life insurance, you should be looking for clients who have just bought a new home, bought a new car, or had a kid. If you are a real estate broker, the life shifts you might be looking for are kids beginning school, divorces, or deaths. If you are an investment advisor, you might be looking for people with job changes. Whatever the case, you should be targeting the demographic that is most likely to need what you are selling.

One of the things MyOutDesk does well is that our sales team, which includes VPs, is a group full of prospecting powerhouses. They work the phones day in, day out, having four hours of conversation each day. Our sales team is just as effective closing cold leads as they are with warm leads because they focus entirely on clients' outcomes.

Learn more here: https://www.MyOutDesk.com/4P.

Presenting

If I were to ask you what presenting involves, what would you say? Your answer would probably be something like, "I start by telling them about my product or service, point out why they should choose me and not someone else, and tell them how customers think my company is stellar in its niche." And there is nothing wrong with that. But what I want you to remember is that presenting should also involve focusing on what is in it for them, the clients. What is their best outcome? We often ask our clients, "If you could have one win out of this call, what would it be? If you could walk away with one thing of value, what is it?" In other words, we help them focus on determining what would be a win for them.

We train our virtual professionals to focus on this. In fact, one of our core values is having a servant heart. We want to serve our clients and vendors we are in business with. Our perspective is that when you add value to people, it will be reciprocated. Focus your presentation on the end users, make sure they are your focus, and help them with their dreams and goals.

Scale Framework: A company mission (what you do), vision (where you are going), values (the standards you collectively hold), value proposition (why clients choose you), and positioning (how your company is different or better) are required when you reach the We Do It stage and can be folded into story mode while presenting and prospecting to a potential client.

Please visit https://www.MyOutDesk.com/Presenting.

Persistent Follow-up

Persistent follow-up really matters, and this is something our virtual professionals excel at. If someone isn't moving forward with your product, you need to find out why. The other day, my wife and I were talking about moving our girls into one of our second-story bedrooms. I thought bunk beds might be a good solution for them, but my wife wasn't sure that they would be big enough to handle that yet.

I did a quick Google search for bunk beds to see if that was the case, and naturally, within minutes, Facebook had placed ads for bunk beds in my feed. It's amazing how that works, isn't it? Facebook knows what is going on in our world. Even though we aren't quite ready for bunk beds yet, as long as that ad campaign continues in my feed, I will probably click through to look at them—because, guess what? Next year, I will be ready to buy bunk beds. It is the same with following up; if a potential client is not ready to buy yet, establish a date when they might be. Next Christmastime, for example, might be a good time to get me thinking about bunk beds again.

This is massively important for our salespeople because we have instilled the notion in them that 90 percent of the time, there is no way to know why someone isn't buying unless you ask.

Potential Referrals

The last of the 4Ps is the potential referral. I don't like to lose, so if I find that a person just isn't ready to move forward with me (or even if they do move forward), I like to say, "Hey, I hope you found value in our conversation today. Who are the two or three people you like and admire who would enjoy a conversation like the one you and I just had?" I am ready to write people's names down, and often ask for a personal email introduction to warm things up. For any business owner aiming for a 70 percent referral rate, this can transition your company directly into hypergrowth and scaling.

Scale Framework: Visit our website for a video explanation of this framework at https://www.MyOutDesk.com/4P.

Chapter 10

The 3Rs

Another mnemonic I'd like you to remember that will help you and your team stay firmly in the dollar-productive zone is the 3Rs: Referral Strategies, Recommendations, and Reviews. Why is this important? Recently we began to ask our clients via text and email this question: "What is the one reason you choose to do business with MyOutDesk?"

We received several different responses. We next asked everyone to choose one from the top three responses we'd received. Overwhelmingly, our clients reported that they choose us because of the quality of talent we provide (which allows our clients to scale). The two runner-up reasons were that we are the price leaders in our industry and that they know and trust MyOutDesk because of our ten-year history and client track record.

Scale Accelerator: Go to https://www.MyOutDesk.com/Sales to get a copy of our surveys, questions we ask clients to focus our marketing message, and more strategies on driving sales with a virtual professional.

How do we know this? Because MyOutDesk cares, and so we asked our clients. Because we listen to our clients. Because of this strategy: the 3Rs!

The 3Rs

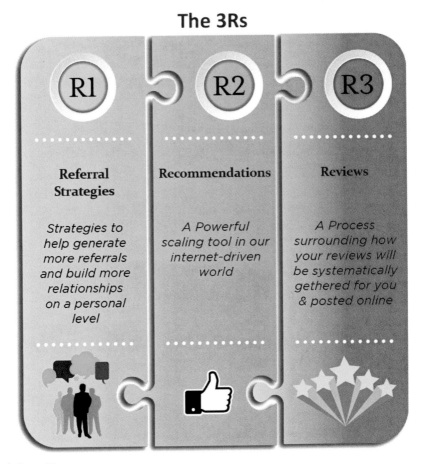

Figure 17.

Referral Strategies

We have already discussed the importance of referrals in scaling your business to the seven-figure level. It's about building relationships on a personal level, but that doesn't mean it can't be systematized. Having a referral strategy is something that many substage one, two, or three business owners have never considered before, but it is such a crucial aspect of the 7-Figure Business Roadmap. Our team has systemwide, automated referral reminders built into the client portal. We also have specific virtual professional and client touchpoints that remind them how much we value referrals. We expect our clients and virtual professionals to refer three people to MyOutDesk within the first ninety days of doing business, and this expectation is set from the start of the sales process.

Recommendations

Having a system around recommendations is a powerful scaling tool in our internet-driven world. You can use testimonial-style recommendations on your website and social media pages to bolster the public image of your company. You should always be nurturing your online presence, and the great news is virtual professionals can do much of this work for you. MyOutDesk has an automated touchpoint that generates recommendations. It regularly surveys our clients and virtual professionals for net promoter scores (a management tool that can be used to gauge customer relationships), produces client/virtual professional video testimonials, and creates focus groups as part of our Because We Listen and Deliver program. We have a robust reporting structure around the 3Rs and can use it as a predictable statistical data set.

Reviews

Reviews are vital to just about any business today. Reviews drive so much business, and you must have a process surrounding how yours will be systematically gathered for you and posted online. Your VPs can be pursuing reviews in their communications with clients. There are also automated email tools that can ask for reviews with a quick "Hey, give me a couple of sentences. Tell me what you think." Your VPs can help you manage sharing those reviews. Once you generate great reviews, they have lasting value; they are viewed over and over again by potential customers, driving revenue back to your business.

We have a process in place so that when someone says that our VPs amaze him or her, we point that person to an area to do an online review. There will be specific sites you will want to be well represented on. These days, you can pick up your iPhone and ask Siri, "Who's the best real estate agent in Yorba Linda, California?" or "Where is the best restaurant near me?" Siri and other search tools gather that information from sites like Yelp and Google, so you have to make sure you have a presence on those tools to the best possible degree.

We Are a Sales Organization

The reason the 3Rs and 4Ps are so important is that in order to take the next step on the 7-Figure Business Roadmap, every employee you have must somehow be involved in the identification, attraction, and retention of customers. That is the path to growth and scaling. What we do at

MyOutDesk isn't just selling the services of virtual professionals; we are selling you the ability to close more business in a year. We are selling an opportunity to fast-track the growth of your company and scale.

Even though taking on virtual professionals may seem like an increase in overhead at first, every dollar you spend on virtual professionals will add at least three dollars to your bottom line (some of our clients have said the return is as much as eight times each dollar spent). Once your team is in place, you should work to ensure that what is paramount to every single employee is to directly get and keep customers, with no exceptions. If you allow your team to focus too much on all the little details and take their eyes off getting and keeping customers, that is precisely what you will get: everything but customers.

Real-Life Success Story: Everyone Is in Sales in Sam's Business

Sam is a businessman in Southern California who has reduced his business success to one simple matrix: recruitment of salespeople. Sam's entire business model makes sense only if his head count is over one thousand salespeople, and so he focused 100 percent of his efforts on internal referrals for more salespeople, creating a referral prize for his existing team members: a Mercedes. Any person inside his company who brings a new salesperson to his office is entered into a raffle with a prize of the company paying the referring person's lease payment for three years, up to $600 a month.

In 2017, Sam grew his firm by over 100 percent using this referral strategy; in 2018, his salesperson head count grew to eight hundred agents (very close to his goal of one thousand). The cost is $5,000, and he had close to two hundred new agents join his team due to this one referral strategy. Why is this important? Every person inside Sam's organization is in sales and provides referrals. Imagine if inside your organization you could have everyone from your front-desk guy to the account team to your operations team engaged in getting new customers and keeping customers.

Scale Framework: Using the models just described, work out the one thing inside your business to focus on. Prioritize the possibilities using the priority matrix. Scale your business by focusing your entire team, as Sam did, on that one area of focus. Visit https://www.MyOutDesk.com/Framework. You may also want to visit https://www.MyOutDesk.com/Accelerator.

Chapter 11

The MOD Growth Stack

You may have heard the term "growth stack," a set of tools and processes teams use to drive growth, in the business sphere in recent years. At the center of our growth stack, like everything else we do, is outcomes.

When a job needs to be done, and you ask MyOutDesk to fill that need for you, we craft an outcome statement for that role. The outcome statement replaces a job description, key area roles and responsibilities, and all those outdated concepts that most businesses still work with when they hire. We prefer the outcome statement as a guide because it yields an important success factor: a measurable result.

Once the outcome statement has been crafted, we send it to our placements team, whose members go to the market to find a committed talent match. They look for someone who can fulfill that outcome statement for you and feel comfortable doing the job. Then we send along videos, personality profiles, and resumes, and ultimately put that person in front of you for a face-to-face video interview.

Once someone is selected for that outcome statement, we help you craft the perfect onboarding program for him or her. In chapter 15, I share our Virtual Playbook, which is part of that process. Usually, there is a 180-day launch period in which you are focused on getting that person up to speed as quickly as possible. In the beginning, a new employee has a lower value for an entrepreneur because of the time you must invest in training. Over time, his or her value goes up, while the work for you associated with that person continues to go down. Typically, the professional's value and the value of your time converge at about the 180-day mark. At that point, you will feel relief and you will begin to see your outcomes come alive.

The challenge is that there is a J-curve in the beginning of the onboarding process. The person being onboarded doesn't really know your business or understand your value proposition to the world yet. He or she hasn't internalized your style of doing business or even the product or service that you offer. Even if the person has fulfilled similar outcomes in other jobs before, that person may not yet understand your unique business. At the 180-day point, your new employee tends to be through the downward slope of the J-curve and beginning to propel upward. Once that occurs, scaling and purpose become the things you can hyper-focus on.

Scaling occurs organically when the VP is in place. Your VP has taken away the busywork that isn't growing your company and driving revenue at this point, so you can move forward and scale. You are able to refocus your attention on the things that matter.

In addition to that, you now have renewed purpose in your business. You are having an impact every time you give someone a job. You are giving the VP's family income, health care, and vacation time, and you are contributing to our nonprofit efforts. You will experience that once you have a couple of VPs in place, you will experience more and more opportunities to reach back out to our placements team and say, "I need another outcome reached." That's scaling at work, and it is what the MOD Growth Stack is all about. Your business will have a first-growth phase, and once you've experienced our virtual talent, you'll see it as an opportunity to continue up the scaling path. We are the resource you will go to when you begin to ask, "Who do I need in order to grow?" We have helped businesses in the insurance, residential services, health and wellness, real estate, mortgage, technology, and professional services industries scale this way.

Scale Accelerator: If you want to know more, visit our website at https://www.MyOutDesk.com/SignUp and schedule a free consultation.

Chapter 12

Sales Development Virtual Professionals

About 50 percent of the virtual professionals we place with clients are fulfilling clients' sales development outcomes. That means about two thousand five hundred of the five thousand virtual professionals we have introduced to clients have been working in sales. Through that experience, we have garnered a lot of evidence about how best to prepare virtual professionals for sales—and we have created a concrete system to ensure that you have success with yours too.

Virtual professionals can help you and your business enormously when it comes to generating and converting leads, that is, taking a potential customer who may have an interest in your business, or even may never have heard of your business, and turning that lead into a warm opportunity. That warm opportunity would include a sales meeting, and if all goes well, a sales quote. Preparing virtual professionals to succeed with this outcome is one of my favorite things to do because the path to having your investment in sales development reps (SDR) pay off in terms of revenue is clear-cut and highly measurable from an outcome basis.

When I say pay off, I'm not speaking merely of an increase in sales. In business, I like a three-to-one return. If I'm spending $5,000 to put someone in place, I want to see a $15,000 return. Your top concern about onboarding a virtual sales team will probably be "How do I do this?" Well, you could just put someone in a seat and say, "OK, now go sell for me," and ask that individual to be accountable for some metrics you have made up in your head. In fact, as an entrepreneur, your go-to mode is probably that you jump right in first and worry about the how later. That is classic entrepreneur behavior, and in general, it's a great attribute. In this instance, however, I'd like you to resist that and reframe your thinking.

This is a situation in which having a concrete plan will pay off in real dollars. Think about onboarding an SDR as if you are running a relay race and you have a baton in your hand. You're fully committed, and you're killing it at Usain Bolt speed. As you approach runner number two, she holds out her hand expectantly to receive the baton. But instead of passing it to her, you throw it to her. It misses its mark, striking her in the head, and she stumbles. Not smart, right? You have just set up your talented teammate to fail. And that is the biggest mistake that people make when they hire VPs: They chuck the baton rather than smoothly hand it off. So, all you need is a recipe for a smooth handoff.

Have Bulletproof Scripts

Scripts are in the virtual professional's arsenal. Here are the elements you should painstakingly document in written form for your new sales team members. Of course, the content will vary depending on the type of business you are in, but for the moment, I will give you examples based on what we use at MyOutDesk.

A Clear Elevator Pitch

Know your elevator pitch. The base formula for a good elevator pitch is "I serve [who] to do [what], so they [get this result]." Ours is: "We instantly scale growing companies with virtual professionals." That is what we do at MyOutDesk, in a nutshell. The elevator pitch is such an important piece for you to craft and for your VPs to absorb. You all need to be on the same page as you communicate your company's value, and once you have articulated this clearly and documented it transparently, your VPs will be able to advance that message. They will communicate it in exactly the way you would.

Know Your Value Proposition

This might seem a bit obvious, but many business owners think their value proposition is just that—obvious—and they fail to document it concretely for their virtual sales reps. Give them the information they need to be

Have a Positioning Document

A positioning document expresses how your product or service fills a need that competitors don't, so this is a critical piece for a sales development rep to know. At MyOutDesk, our positioning document has expressions along these lines:

1. We have helped over five thousand clients grow their businesses.
2. We make sure that every virtual professional you interview is exceptional and MOD-certified because of our thorough vetting process.
3. We have been in this business for twelve years and built an industry around serving medium and small businesses.
4. We provide market-force personality profiles to accurately match talent.
5. We provide medical benefits, microloans, vacations, and conferences for our virtual professionals.
6. MyTimeIn is our proprietary software that helps track outcomes and provides daily task oversight.
7. We have a Chief People Office in the United States that personally vets our virtual professionals.
8. Your partnership with us benefits our Charity Impact Movement (503c). We give away thousands of dollars every year to impoverished communities.

These are points on which none of our competitors can compare. Anyone who tries to stack up against that will have a huge challenge, and the only way they can win is through offering a lower price and lower quality. MyOutDesk is the price leader and has the highest quality available, so this is exactly where I want our competitors to be (a lower-priced alternative). If they offer lower prices, we can say, "Look at all the value we have to help your business scale. If you are looking for the cheapest, that's not us. If you are looking to scale effectively, while ensuring a great end product that gives value to your customers, we know how to do that."

clear in their conversations about why your clients choose you. What is the benefit they see? We hear time and time again from our clients that they are overwhelmed, and alleviating that overwhelm is where we add massive value. They are so busy, and we are the "easy button" for finding talent to help them. There is no way they could find five people to interview in forty-eight hours...but we can. We have already vetted them. The MyOutDesk value proposition: "We provide indispensable VPs to growing businesses." If you can articulate your value proposition clearly to your virtual professionals and have that in written form somewhere they can refer to, you are hitting one out of the park from the outset.

Have a Process for Handling Objections

When you give your virtual professionals your value proposition, you are giving them the ideal outcome. But you also have to prepare them for the challenges they'll encounter. Document all the objections that a potential customer might have for your product or service, and your virtual professionals will wear it like armor in their conversations with leads. They will be ready to answer potential customers' objections in a friendly way. Why might a customer say no? What answer could your virtual professionals give that might turn that into a yes? Help them to anticipate these issues.

The Most Common Objections at MyOutDesk:

1. *What about internet connections there in the Philippines?* Our answer to this is that all our virtual professionals have a 5MB connection and a 2MB backup connection.
2. *What about their English?* Well, there is a reason we chose the Philippines. It's the number one outsourcing country in the world, which means that there are literally millions of educated people there who speak great English and who are serving companies like yours right now. You are in the right place.
3. *How do I know my virtual professionals are really working on my projects?* We have our own tracking software. You can log in to it and see their screenshots and what websites they go to.

4. *Do they work my work hours?* Yes, they will work your normal business hours.

5. *How can you possibly vet these people from all the way over there?* Well, we do dual-vetting because we are an entity in the United States and in the Philippines. We do an FBI-grade background check and verify all experience and qualifications.

And so on. Documenting both your value proposition (why customers say yes) and the possible objections (why customers say no) is the one area in which most business owners mess up. They don't document this stuff and place it where it is transparent for everybody, and this sets up VPs to fail. Set yours up to win by spending some time crafting these important pieces.

Download our troubleshooting examples: https://www .MyOutDesk.com/SDRexamples.

Have a System for Measuring Results

You and your sales virtual professionals will know you are scaling the business when you have clearly defined processes for measuring the following:

1. Leads received: This is the number one thing you must track. How many leads are coming into your business every single day, week, and month?

2. Number of calls: How many calls did your virtual professionals make to those leads?

3. Leads converted: How many of those calls went from being just a lead to an actual opportunity to sell?

4. Speed to lead: This is a metric that really matters. How much time elapses between when the lead comes in to when the call goes out, and does it convert successfully? For example, a lead might come in at 1:00, and they get a call five minutes later.

5. New clients/sales: How many new clients resulted from this process? This is the bottom line. Have a system in place that tracks all these things in a way that is easy for everyone to understand.

Avoid These Failure Points

What I have described so far are the things you need to do to be successful in scaling with your virtual SDRs. Based on my vast experience, I'd also like to give you come common pitfalls to avoid.

1. **You don't have enough leads:** I like to have five hundred new leads a month, but your number will depend on what industry you are in and what your sales cycle looks like. I always like to have three to five salespeople behind our virtual SDRs. An SDR's job is to convert a lead into an opportunity, right? And the salesperson's job is to turn that opportunity into a client. It is important for the SDR to feel like he or she is on the same team with the salesperson, and vice versa. Having enough leads and enough salespeople allows you to test who is closing and who is not. We once had a client come to us because he was upset his team wasn't converting enough leads. It turned out that the salesperson wasn't immediately calling the leads once they got converted into an opportunity, instead letting them go for two or three days before calling. It's very important that you have enough people and a measurement for speed to lead for both the VP and the salesperson here in the United States.

2. **You aren't doing daily and weekly meetings:** I like a daily morning meeting with a little music and a little coffee, so everyone can talk about the wins. Everyone is talking about where their energy is and how they are feeling, and we are putting positivity out early in the morning so that feeling can be conveyed through the phones. Weekly meetings are for making commitments to sales and conversation goals.

3. **You aren't tracking conversations:** Someone who is having forty or fifty conversations per day is going to have a different result than someone who is having ten. You want to set concrete goals for the number of conversations and share those in your daily and weekly meetings.

4. **You don't have activity-level measurements:** Your system for measuring results should include everyone on your team. How many calls did each person make? How many times did each person try? How fast did each person handle the opportunities in front of him or her, and how often convert? These are important metrics to have for each individual.

5. **You aren't going after the 3Rs:** As I mentioned in chapter 11, referrals, recommendations, and reviews are critical to your business. It is astounding how many businesses fail to harness the power of these three things. We chase them ruthlessly at MyOutDesk. In fact, we get referrals all the time from people who have never even done business with us. There is a woman in Texas who has sent us three or four clients. I had only one conversation with her, five years ago, and she hasn't bought from us, but she keeps sending us people because I had a great conversation with her.

   If you aren't pursuing the 3Rs with your team, you are missing out. As you can see, my prevailing message about how to set up your virtual SDRs for success is communicate, communicate, communicate. Assume nothing, and document everything.

Scale Accelerator: For a complete guide to setting up a two-step sales process that all major companies use, go to https://www.MyOutDesk.com/SDRexamples. We provide a spreadsheet, accountability matrix, technology systems, and a full guide to using an SDR inside your business to scale.

Chapter 13

Virtual Marketing Professionals

All the information I asked you to document in the last chapter to help you scale with virtual SDRs also applies to virtual marketing coordinators and marketing design professionals. When marketing professionals have an ironclad understanding of your elevator pitch, value proposition, and positioning documents, they can distill that message down for social media, video, photos, infographics, and really all kinds of things that help them to market your product or service and your message.

Also, if they have a clear idea of potential objections your customers might have, they can subtly address those through their work. Having those written pieces as concrete, concise, and clear as possible will yield as much benefit for marketing professionals as it will for sales professionals.

With this understanding about your company's message in place, there are many things a virtual marketing professional can do for you to supercharge your company's scalability. Focus your talented marketing professionals on the above sales tools and on ideal client targets. If you know who buys from you and why, your marketing virtual professional can really help drive your message out to the marketplace.

Branding

I have already shared with you that it was my first VP, Lily, who designed our MyOutDesk logo and put it into action. We have discovered that printing that logo on signs and banners can be a very powerful tool for

Our logo goes all over the world!

VPs are great at design coordination, including the banners for our conference.

our business. Among our own folks, whenever they go on vacation or have something amazing happen, they will pull out one of our banners and snap a picture, saying, "Thank you, MyOutDesk for helping us do this!" We have thousands of people carrying around our banner, and it is very powerful. They show up on Facebook, in text messages, and in thank-you cards. This is an example of the kind of marketing collateral and professional branding those virtual marketing professionals can create for you.

Design Coordination

Above is an example of a marketing piece we have done for our company. Your virtual design coordinators can put together pieces like this, so you can promote your business with clarity out in the world. This is a banner from our company fiesta where we had more than a thousand VP and their families show up to celebrate our ten-year anniversary. It was a very special event.

Repurposing Content

One virtual marketing coordinator role that will benefit your business is re-purposing content. When you create a blog post, for example, and put it on your website, you can have someone repurpose that content and multiply its effect. You can tweet about it. You can put it on LinkedIn. You can send video content to YouTube. There are so many ways your unique content can be pro-liferated out in the world when you have someone to do that cyber-legwork for you. If there is a call to action to schedule a consultation, to subscribe to a newsletter, to get more information, to download something, or to do what-ever your lead-gathering strategy might be, your marketing coordinator can put more eyes on it. This is a tried-and-true driver of new business.

Events

I love client referral events. Having your VPs track referral events can be a huge part of your growth. If your business is operating well, you probably have 25 to 50 percent of your business coming from referrals, but as an entrepreneur and business owner, tracking them is not necessarily something you should be spending your time on. Ask a VP do it for you.

Social Media

Social media has gone from being a useful business tool to a critical and mandatory focus in recent years. Every social media platform has a different format, and that means it takes time, energy, and effort to create different content for those formats. There is a medium for every form of content, and we have VPs who are expert at optimizing your exposure through those platforms for you.

For example, let's say you have five thousand Facebook friends. How do you know that these are the best five thousand to have? You can have your virtual professional put them through a process where people you've engaged with are coming up more and more on your screen. You're driving more and more referrals through your community and creating posts in return. Seemingly overnight, you are a bit of a local celebrity! But again, you don't want social media to consume your own time, so you can delegate it to a VP.

Daniel Ramsey shared MyOutDesk, LLC.'s live video.
23 hrs ·

JOIN US LIVE in this FREE WEBINAR: Double your listings in low inventory markets with Landvoice Christoph and Jonathon

Marketing Automation

Marketing automation is a very big deal and is a vital aspect of scaling along the 7-Figure Business Roadmap. Everyone at the They Do It stage has some sort of marketing automation in place. Running a marketing automation system involves a lot of work inputting information into a CRM application, setting up email campaigns, and setting up drip campaigns. Luckily, all that can be done virtually as well.

Impressed with what our sales and marketing virtual professionals can do? Wait until you see how operations and administrative professionals can transform your business.

Check out our Marketing VP Guide: https://www.MyOutDesk .com/Repurpose.

Chapter 14

Administrative Virtual Professionals

Your Sticky Challenge will have convinced you that one of the keys to scaling is to remove yourself from the administrative activities of your business and to focus your time on growing your company. Having a VP tackle operations and administrative outcomes for you can go far beyond what a traditional assistant does, like answering phones and keeping your calendar. There are many more ways a VP can help you administratively. Here are some concrete examples of my favorite things administrative VPs do for our clients.

Lead Management

Figure 18, from early 2018, shows what MyOutDesk has in place so that sales and marketing can know how we have handled a hotline, a web chat, or an email campaign lead coming into our CRM.

When someone comes to MyOutDesk who is interested in working with us, we have a script and a completely outlined lead process in hand. While all salespeople need to embrace those standard operating procedures, they don't necessarily need to be the ones who own those documents; you could have an administrative VP who acts as that owner and keeper of these very important procedures and process. You will be amazed at how having someone to do this will keep you from getting bogged down with the sales side of your business.

Lead Process

PURPOSE
To achieve efficiency, quality result and aligned performance while reducing miscommunication and failure to comply in MyOutDesk's standards in managing and processing leads.

GROUPS INVOLVED
1. Marketing and Sales Department
    a. Sales Development Representative (SDR)
    b. Sales Representative (SR)

TYPES OF LEADS
1. Real Estate (RE)
2. Other (new verticals)
    a. Residential   d. Professional Services
    b. Health and Wellness   e. Technology
    c. Insurance
3. Partner

SALES STAGES FOR LEADS TAGGED AS REAL ESTATE AND OTHER
1. Prequalification Stage
2. Scheduling Appointment
3. Strategy Session
4. Second Level Qualification
5. Client Service Agreement

NEW LEADS
New Leads will mostly come from Marketo. The following information will be transferred to Salesforce:

1. Prequalification Stage   4. Phone
2. Scheduling Appointment   5. Lead Source
3. Strategy Session   6. Lead Source Detail

Figure 18.

Lead Reporting

One opportunity many business owners overlook is taking advantage of all the reporting and business analytics virtual professionals can provide. Here is a report prepared for one of our clients. In it, you can see a lot of information: where revenue came from during this reporting period, how many deals were closed, what expenses there were, and what conversion rates looked like. Numbers like these can be prepared for you so you can know where to best spend your marketing dollars and how you can be most effective in closing deals. (See figure 19.)

Net Promoter Scores

Another thing your VPs can do for you is to keep track of net promoter scores. Whenever we have asked clients, "How likely are you to refer colleagues and friends to our service?" and the answer is "Very likely," or, "Not likely," we know that those who say "not likely" are clients we need to focus on. They are, in a way, raising their hands and saying, "Hey, we are not 100 percent happy," and finding out why yields useful information. A VP can track both the "likely" responders and the "unlikely," over time, to see if the same issues keep coming up and to report back to you about how more customers can become likely to give you a referral. Many companies don't have a quality score around their service or product, and having an administrative professional to survey clients, employees, and vendors is a great way to get feedback you can use to implement long-term structural changes.

Recruitment

I'm an employer, and we have thousands of folks who work for MyOutDesk. I know from experience that sorting through all the applications we get is a big challenge and not necessarily the best use of my time as an entrepreneur. We have had years when we had over thirty thousand applicants for only five hundred jobs. As you would imagine, the process of narrowing the field to the two thousand or so viable candidates we would want to interview is daunting. As a business owner, it is your job to interview and find talent, but posting jobs and screening the multitudes are not. This is something that an administrative professional can handle for you, when you give that person a clear idea of what your criteria are. This will save you time and energy while allowing you to focus on revenue-producing activities.

2019 Yearly Media Source Summary

		Jan	Feb	Mar	Apr	May	Jun	Jul	Aug	Sep	Oct
TRADITIONAL MARKETING		O	O	O	O	O	O	O	O	O	O
1	Brochure Back										
2	Brochure Front										
3	Glenn Beck/Guaranteed Sale										
4	Home Again										
5	Radio Show										
6	Realtor										
7	Seminars										
8	Sign										
9	Sign Calls										
10	Top Marketer										
11	Walk In										
INTERNET MARKETING		O	O	O	O	O	O	O	O	O	O
	Agent Panel Gold										
	BoomTown										
	Craigslist										
	Dave Ramsey										
	Trulia										
	Tulia,Zillow										
	Zbuyer										
	Zillow.com paid										
	Zopim										
PROSPECTING		O	O	O	O	O	O	O	O	O	O
	Expired/Red X										
	Open Houses										
OLD MARKETING		O	O	O	O	O	O	O	O	O	O
TOTAL		O	O	O	O	O	O	O	O	O	O
DC Opportunities											
DC Answered											
Telepro Minutes											
Telepro Dials											
Telepro Contacts											
Telepro Appointments											
Telepro Listings Ref											

Figure 19.

Agent Onboarding

Sprint Start Date:			Sprint Due Date:		
Importance	Status	Objective	Notes		Assign To
1000		Team Leader to send email notifying that New Agent is starting	provides start date, time		
995		Put Agent info in CRM	Agent Onboarding: How Tos: Adding an Agent into CRM		
990		Support starts onboarding process	Agent Onboarding Checklist		
988		Support sends standard welcome email to New Agent	Welcome email to Agent		
985		Support looks up New Agent License number	Look up by name—get license number		
983		If Agent is still listed under old agency, check back to see when freed	Check back 2x a day and update Agent each time		
981		Register license	Step-by-step guide in onboarding folder in drive		
980		Notify MLS of new affiliate	Insert MLS contact		
978		Create a New Agent folder for all documents	Put all docs, signed contracts, etc., in here		
975		Procure copy of RE license	Give to Team Leader for file in office		
970		Procure 2 New Agent Bios (4-line and 5-line)	Save example to show		
965		Procure professional picture of New Agent for business card			
963		Confirms New Agent has smartphone			
960		Confirm receipt of required docs	Onboarding completed required documents		
955		Confirm all docs have been saved to New Agent folder			

Figure 20.

Agile Project Management

Agile project management is a great way to use your virtual administrative professionals. Following is an example of a spreadsheet that could represent project management for anyone on your team. On the left side, you can score the importance of the task, starting at 1,000 and going down so that the highest tasks go to the top and the lowest go to the bottom. For each task, you can assign objectives, due dates, the person(s) who will handle it, documentation needed and completion dates. These can all be housed in one spot. (See figure 20.)

If you are running a big organization and you have as many events as MyOutDesk does (for example, we might have a birthday party this week, a client event next week, and a team-building event coming up next month). All the related details have to be tracked as a project. There are the flights, the hotels, the venue details and schedules…and all of this can be managed by VPs. Many of our clients and VPs use the Basecamp app to run complex, multifunctional projects. Some still use a simple Excel spreadsheet, like the one I share here. Others use a kind of software that is specific to project management. Whatever you use, you can give it to a virtual professional to run it for you.

Performance Reporting

Performance reporting is another role that virtual administrative professionals can assume. Here is an example from several years ago of our incoming leads, where they came from, and how many converted across different departments. A VP compiled that information and maintained it over time so we could have access to that data. (See figure 21.)

There are many different access points VPs can have for this kind of data. If you have a phone system, there is a back end for that phone system from which data can be pulled. If you have a CRM, there is a back end for that from which you can extract how many leads came in and what the activity looks like. If you have some sort of delivery software in which you are running projects, you can pull that data out of the back end. If you have financials, you can tie the operations of your business back to those financials. These are all examples of performance reporting. A VP will have to be given resources to do this; this person won't be able to jump straight in and know how to do it. But once it is set up, and you have introduced the process, your VP will be able to maintain it for you and report back in a consistent format.

Customer Support

In chapter 3, I mentioned Chris, a VP at MyOutDesk who has been supporting our client Knolly William's technology company. The technology is a CRM. A few years ago, Knolly hadn't been sure what he was going to do with his tech company. He was going to either ditch it or move forward with it. It had an inexpensive price point, so there were a lot of potential users, and it was a recurring source of revenue for him. The problem was

SUMMARY	7-Aug	8-Aug	9-Aug	Total Number of Outgoing Calls for the Month	Total Number of Contacts Made for the Week (Contacts Made, Nurture and Transfers)
Number of Outgoing Calls	57	19	138	214	58
Number of Contacts Made	26	11	5		
Nurture	1	0	2	3	
Number of Voice Mails	27	6	66		
Number of Wrong Numbers	0	0	0		
Number of No Contacts	1	1	65		
Number of Appointments	2	1	0	3	
Number of Contacts (Contacts Made, Nurture and Appointment)	29	12	7		
	57	19	138		

Figure 21.

that he was tired of working on it himself as a business owner. I told him I could get him somebody to help.

That's where Chris came in. He is the customer support touch point for all inquiries, sales, and operations. The only things he doesn't handle are speaking engagements, writing about the CRM, and working with the tech people to maintain and develop the technology. Knolly does all of that. But Chris handles everything else, from onboarding to helping someone move his or her CRM from an old system. Chris feels like a partner to Knolly, and he loves his work. He is a great example of an administrative VP who has made a business come alive.

Scale Framework: Go to https://www.MyOutDesk.com /AdministrativeVP to get copies of all of the examples in this chapter and a short video on how to implement a VP in your administrative team.

Chapter 15

The Virtual Playbook

One of the things that worries business owners as they begin to work with VPs is how to handle mistakes when they are made. When employees are in the office with you, you can talk to them immediately and directly. It's natural to worry about how you will make that same connection with someone who might be thousands of miles away—in our case, a fourteen-hour plane flight away.

That is why we recommend that everyone craft a Virtual Playbook. You will be amazed at how efficiently you can achieve your outcomes when you have a play-by-play, documented process for dealing with training and what to do when something goes wrong. It takes all the guesswork out of the employer-employee relationship. How do you do that? How do you make sure that your virtual professionals have all the tools they need to be successful in this blended model?

The answer is beautifully simple: You document your systems. Within your scale framework, when a virtual professional makes a mistake, there must be a process for determining why. As an entrepreneur, you might tend to be upset when someone makes a mistake. You might think, "How could my virtual professional make such a needless mistake? This isn't working. You made a bad experience occur for my client, and I can't believe you did that." The tendency of an entrepreneur is to blame the employee because we believe we would have done things differently.

The first question you should ask yourself is "Do I have a written process in my standard operating procedures on how to do this task (or confront this issue)?" The standard operating procedures (SOP) should be sufficiently complete to guide your VP through everything to be touched within the business, even if it is as trivial as how to answer the phone, where to store documents, or what to put in an email signature. Then, when someone comes on board, that new employee has a reference point for everything about the job.

The second question you should ask yourself is "Did I conduct formal training on how to do that?" You can't simply give someone a written procedure and say, "Here you go. Good luck." You must help the person understand why the procedure is to be done and then further clarify by answering any questions that arise.

If you answer yes to both those questions, you can go back through that documentation with the employee and show how you covered that scenario in the training process. This gives the employee the opportunity to say, "Gosh, you are right. I do remember that in the training. It's my mistake, and it won't happen again." Tell your employee, "Great, I'm so glad that we are clear about this. Thank you for your commitment that it won't happen again."

With all your documentation in place, you can put the onus on the employee to realize the mistake, and by asking yourself the right questions, you avoid making unpleasant and counterproductive assumptions, like "They should have known that." Plus, you enable a future where that mistake won't happen again and again and again.

SOP Framework: Go to https://www.MyOutDesk.com /SOPframework for more information about the framework.

Play, Pause, Do

The process of doing that virtually is something we call Play, Pause, Do. This is where you take a written standard operating procedure and record a screen share that shows you actually doing the activity. Now not only are you seen doing the activity but you can talk to your employees about it and answer questions about why you are doing it.

Play, Pause, Do requires a video be associated with the written documentation for every standard operating procedure. Play, Pause, Do allows an employee who may have gone through two weeks of training several months ago to go back to the procedures and be able to complete tasks more successfully.

The great thing is that once you have a video recording of something, it lives forever. You have crafted it, and it can be set on a Vimeo or YouTube account and played back as much as is needed. These accounts can be set to "private" so that only people with company email addresses, for example, can access them.

Why is all this documentation so important? So little of human communication is fully understood in a single iteration. Only 55 percent of face-to-face communication is fully understood. That means that 45 percent of the time, people don't correctly understand you, even if you are standing right in front of them! What's more, only 37 percent of nonvisual verbal communication and 17 percent of written communication is fully understood. Isn't that astounding? Quite literally, 83 percent of the time you can expect your emails to be misunderstood. It is a natural human failing that can be overcome only by repetition and clarification.

Accept that, because going throughout the world thinking, "Well, I told them," will not help you scale. The onus is on you, the business owner and chief communicator, to provide clarity if you want to be successful.

One of the hardest pills I had to swallow was understanding that my adult learners need to hear something, on average, seven times before they fully can appreciate and implement a new change inside of a business. You might be thinking, "Well, I don't hire average, Daniel," and perhaps that's true, but even if you get someone twice as adapt and intelligent, you'll need to make sure there are several reminders, perhaps three to four reinforcements, of a new concept. To be perfectly frank, while this book is to help our clients learn best practices, it also serves a purpose for our internal team here at MyOutDesk. It is a reinforcement point in our understanding of our company's vision and mission.

When you are a business owner in the weeds, so to speak, it may not seem like a good use of your time to document all this training. You might be thinking, "This is a lot of work!" But trust me when I say you will be glad you followed the process to the letter. Once it is done, it can be replicated a thousand times. And it might not even take up as much time as you think. You can record yourself as you go about doing the tasks you want to delegate, like making sales calls, for example. Rather than spending three hours concocting a dummy training scenario, record a video of a real call. Then it doesn't become a lot of work for you and, overall, is less burdensome.

Scale Accelerator: See more of what I mean at https://www .MyOutDesk.com/PlayPauseDo.

The Learning Framework

The Learning Framework is a training process that the military and major engineering companies use. We have adopted it, too, because it is so effective. Few businesses adopt this framework until they reach the They Do It stage, but we encourage you to use it from the We Do It stage onward. It has these principal steps:

1. **Watch.** The new employee simply watches an experienced one.
2. **Practice.** This is a role-play scenario so that the process can be internalized.
3. **Confirm.** The experienced person watches the new employee do the job to confirm that the trainee has learned it correctly.
4. **Master.** The employee eventually goes on to teach someone else to do the job. Bringing it full circle proves the skill has been mastered.

This tried-and-true system will save you a lot of headaches and make your virtual professionals feel secure in the work they are doing for you. Of course, they will still need to refer to your standard operating procedures over time, so it is important to constantly update them. As a business evolves, you may need to make additions, either by editing a document or adding an update to a video.

The bonus is that the personal touch involved in going through this process with a VP sets the stage for good long-term working relationships. The time you invest will ideally result in your virtual professionals feeling good about going along with you on this entrepreneurial journey and get them excited about bringing your product or service to the world.

Scale Framework: Go to https://www.MyOutDesk.com /VirtualPlaybook for more information about our teaching tools..

Communication

1. **Get a communication platform that includes chat, video call, and phone features.** Here at MyOutDesk, we use a platform called RingCentral. After trying several platforms over the years, this system has worked out best for us. Since we outsource to the Philippines, having chat and video calls has benefited us greatly. We can talk "face-to-face" and record these conversations for future reference, as well as easily correspond whenever we need to. We also have a phone feature wherein we can have a number with a Sacramento area code (where our main office is based) that a VP anywhere in the world can use.

2. **Have a task-management system.** A task-management system is a great way to keep track of projects, daily tasks, events, and a slew of other operations in your business. We use monday.com, but there are a lot of different systems available out there like Basecamp, Trello, etc. You can set up your system by team member or department and have each task aligned with corresponding steps; your team can then make regular updates on progress, ask questions, or even seek the help they need from you to remove any roadblocks. This is an excellent way to keep visibility on the daily goings-on in your business and will give you and your VP an easy way to keep each other updated.

Scale Framework: Go to https://www.MyOutDesk.com /CommunicationGuide for more information about our 4-Step Guide to Communicating with a Real Estate Virtual Assistant. Please also visit https://www.MyOutDesk.com/Framework.